BASIC

ENGLISH

GRAMMAR

Third Edition

WORKBOOK
Volume A

Betty Schrampfer Azar
Stacy A. Hagen

Basic English Grammar, Third Edition
Workbook, Volume A

Pearson Education, 10 Bank Street, White Plains, NY 10606

Staff credits: The people who made up the **Basic English Grammar
Workbook, Volume A, Third Edition** team, representing editorial, production,
design, and manufacturing, are Janice L. Baillie, Nancy Flaggman, Margo Grant,
Melissa Leyva, Robert Ruvo, and Pat Wosczyk.

Azar Associates
Shelley Hartle, Editor
Susan Van Etten, Manager

Text design and composition: Carlisle Publishing Services
Text font: 11/13.5 Plantin
Illustrations: Don Martinetti

LONGMAN ON THE **WEB**

Longman.com offers online resources for
teachers and students. Access our Companion
Websites, our online catalog, and our local
offices around the world.

Visit us at **longman.com.**

ISBN: 0-13-184935-2

Printed in the United States of America
3 4 5 6 7 8 9 10-BAH-11 10 09

Contents

PRACTICES

Chapter 3   USING THE SIMPLE PRESENT

PRACTICES

Chapter 4   USING THE PRESENT PROGRESSIVE

Chapter 5   TALKING ABOUT THE PRESENT

Chapter 6   NOUNS AND PRONOUNS

Preface

The *Basic English Grammar Workbook* is a place for students to explore and practice English grammar on their own. All of the exercises have been designed for independent study; they range from the basic to the more challenging to give students a chance to better understand and use English meaningfully and correctly. This book is also a resource for teachers who need exercise material for additional classwork, homework, testing, or individualized instruction.

The *Workbook* is keyed to the explanatory grammar charts found in *Basic English Grammar, Third Edition,* a classroom teaching text for students of English as a second or foreign language.

The answers to the practices can be found in the *Answer Key* in the back of the *Workbook*. Its pages are perforated so they can be detached to make a separate booklet. However, if teachers want to use the *Workbook* as a classroom teaching text, the *Answer Key* can be removed at the beginning of the term.

CHAPTER 1
Using *Be*

◇ **PRACTICE 1. A or AN. (Chart 1-1)**

Directions: Write ***a*** or ***an*** before each word.

1. __*an*__ office		6. _____ animal	
2. _____ boy		7. _____ ear	
3. _____ desk		8. _____ letter	
4. _____ apple		9. _____ motel	
5. _____ city		10. _____ table	

ear

◇ **PRACTICE 2. A or AN. (Chart 1-1)**

Directions: Complete the sentences with ***a*** or ***an***. Then circle if the answer is ***yes*** or ***no***.

horse

1. __*A*__ horse is __*an*__ animal. (yes) no

2. Paris is _____ city. yes no

3. _____ bee is _____ language. yes no

4. Canada is _____ country. yes no

5. _____ cow is _____ insect. yes no

6. English is _____ country. yes no

7. French is _____ language. yes no

8. Africa is _____ continent. yes no

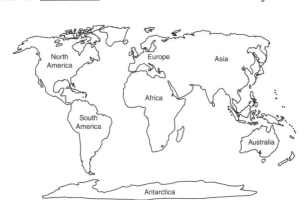

◇ PRACTICE 3. BE. (Chart 1-1)
   Directions: Write complete sentences using **is** and **a/an** and the given words.

   1. A bee \ insect   _____A bee is an insect._____

   2. Chinese \ language   _____

   3. China \ country   _____

   4. Soccer \ sport   _____

   5. A dog \ animal   _____

   6. Bangkok \ city   _____

   7. Thailand \ country   _____

   8. An ant \ insect   _____

◇ PRACTICE 4. Plural nouns. (Chart 1-2)
   Directions: Write the plural forms for the given nouns.

SINGULAR		PLURAL
1. a city	→	_____cities_____
2. a dog	→	_____
3. a language	→	_____
4. a machine	→	_____
5. a country	→	_____
6. a season	→	_____
7. a dictionary	→	_____
8. a vegetable	→	_____

◇ PRACTICE 5. Singular and plural nouns. (Charts 1-1 and 1-2)
   Directions: Complete the words with **-s** or **Ø** (nothing).

   1. A bee __Ø__ is an insect __Ø__ .

   2. Bee _S_ are insect _S_ .

   3. Korean _____ is a language _____ .

   4. A cat _____ is an animal _____ .

   5. Rose _____ are flower _____ .

   6. Spring _____ and summer _____ are season _____ .

   7. Ant _____ are insect _____ .

   8. A cow _____ is an animal _____ .

   9. Soccer _____ and tennis _____ are sport _____ .

◇ **PRACTICE 6. BE with singular and plural. (Charts 1-1 and 1-2)**
Directions: Circle the correct verb.

1. Ants   *is,* ⟨*are*⟩   insects.

2. A chicken   *is, are*   an animal.

3. Chinese and Russian   *is, are*   languages.

4. December and January   *is, are*   months.

5. A computer   *is, are*   a machine.

6. Computers   *is, are*   machines.

7. Bali   *is, are*   an island.

8. Winter   *is, are*   a season.

9. Carrots   *is, are*   vegetables.

10. Indonesia and Malaysia   *is, are*   countries.

11. Horses   *is, are*   animals.

computer

◇ **PRACTICE 7. BE with singular and plural. (Charts 1-1 and 1-2)**
Directions: Complete the sentences with *is* or *are* and one of the nouns in the list. Use the correct singular form of the noun (using *a* or *an*) or the correct plural form.

animal	country	language
city	insect	machine

1. A dog ___*is an animal.*___

2. Dogs ___*are animals.*___

3. Spanish _____.

4. Spanish and Chinese _____.

5. Thailand and Viet Nam _____.

6. Thailand _____.

7. A butterfly _____.

8. Butterflies _____.

9. A car _____.

10. Cars _____.

11. Berlin _____.

12. Berlin and Baghdad _____.

butterfly

◇ PRACTICE 8. BE with singular and plural. (Charts 1-1 and 1-2)
   Directions: Write complete sentences. Use a verb *(is* or *are)*. Use the singular or plural form of the noun.

   1. Asia \ continent   _____Asia is a continent._____

   2. Africa \ continent   _____

   3. Asia and Africa \ continent   _____

   4. Paris \ city   _____

   5. Cairo \ city   _____

   6. Paris and Cairo \ city   _____

   7. Malaysia \ country   _____

   8. Japan and Malaysia \ country _____

◇ PRACTICE 9. Pronoun + BE. (Chart 1-3)
   Directions: Create your own chart by completing the sentences with a form of *be.*

   1. I   _____am____ a student.   6. You
                                                    (two persons) _____ students.
   2. She   _____ a student.
                                                 7. We   _____ students.
   3. He   _____ a student.
                                                 8. You and I   _____ students.
   4. It   _____ a country.
                                                 9. They   _____ students.
   5. You
      (one person) _____ a student.

◇ PRACTICE 10. Pronoun + BE. (Chart 1-3)
   Directions: Complete the sentences with the correct pronouns.

   1. Jack and Bob are teachers. _____They_____ are teachers.

   2. Bob is a teacher. _____ is a teacher.

   3. Susan is a teacher. _____ is a teacher.

   4. Mr. Jones is a teacher. _____ is a teacher.

   5. Mrs. Jones is a teacher. _____ is a teacher.

   6. Mrs. Jones and Mr. Jones are teachers. _____ are teachers.

   7. Mr. Jones and I are teachers. _____ are teachers.

   8. You and I are teachers. _____ are teachers.

   9. Maria is a student. _____ is a student.

10. You and Maria are students. _____ are students.

11. The children are students. _____ are students.

12. Dr. Black is a doctor. Dr. Reed is a doctor. _____ are doctors.

13. Mary is a dentist. _____ is a dentist.

14. Joe is a dentist. _____ is a dentist.

15. Mary, Joe, and I are dentists. _____ are dentists.

dentist

◇ PRACTICE 11. Pronoun + BE. (Chart 1-3)
Directions: Complete the sentences. Use a verb: **am, is,** or **are.** Use a noun: **a student** or **students.**

1. She _____ *is a student* _____.

2. I _____.

3. You (one person) _____.

4. You (two persons) _____.

5. They _____.

6. He _____.

7. We _____.

8. Carlos and you _____.

9. He and I _____.

10. Mia and I _____.

◇ PRACTICE 12. Contractions with BE. (Chart 1-4)
Directions: Write the contractions.

1. I am _____ *I'm* _____

2. he is _____

3. we are _____

4. you are _____

5. they are _____

6. it is _____

7. she is _____

◇ PRACTICE 13. Negative forms of BE. (Chart 1-5)
   Directions: Complete the sentences with the negative form of *be*.

   1. I ____*am not*____ sick.   7. We _____ sick.

   2. You _____ sick.   8. They _____ sick.

   3. He _____ sick.   9. The students _____ sick.

   4. She _____ sick.   10. Katie and I _____ sick.

   5. The cat _____ sick.   11. The teacher _____ sick.

   6. It _____ sick.   12. The teachers _____ sick.

◇ PRACTICE 14. Negative forms of BE and contractions. (Chart 1-5)
   Directions: Complete the sentences with the negative form of *be*. Then write the contracted
   form. Give both forms where possible.

	BE: NEGATIVE		CONTRACTION
1. You	____*are not*____ late.		____*aren't* OR *you're not*____
2. She	_____ late.		_____
3. I	_____ late.		_____
4. He	_____ late.		_____
5. The bus	_____ late.		_____
6. It	_____ late.		_____
7. We	_____ late.		_____
8. You	_____ late.		_____
9. They	_____ late.		_____

◇ PRACTICE 15. Using IS, ISN'T, ARE, or AREN'T. (Chart 1-5)
   Directions: Complete the sentences with *is, isn't, are,* or *aren't*.

   1. Canada and Sweden ____*aren't*____ continents.

   2. Japan _____ a language.

   3. A fly _____ an insect.

   4. Tennis _____ a sport.

   5. Bees _____ insects.

   6. Carrots _____ animals.

7. A rabbit _____ an animal.

8. Seoul _____ a country.

9. North America _____ a continent.

10. Greenland _____ a city.

◇ PRACTICE 16. Using BE. (Chart 1-5)
Directions: Complete the sentences with the correct information. Use a form of **be** with a contraction.

1. Korea _____*isn't*_____ a city. It *'s a country* _____.

2. Computers _____ insects. They _____.

3. Asia _____ a continent. It _____ a country.

4. Spring and summer _____ sports. They _____.

5. Arabic _____ a country. It _____.

6. I _____ an English teacher. I _____.

7. We _____ students. We _____ English teachers.

◇ PRACTICE 17. BE + adjective. (Chart 1-6)
Directions: Complete the sentences with the correct information. Use **is, isn't, are,** or **aren't**.

1. A mouse _____*isn't*_____ big.

2. A diamond _____ cheap.

3. Diamonds _____ expensive.

4. Bananas _____ expensive.

5. The earth _____ flat. It _____ round.

6. English grammar _____ hard. It _____ easy.

7. This exercise _____ difficult. It _____ easy.

8. Flowers _____ ugly. They _____ beautiful.

9. Traffic at rush hour _____ noisy. It _____ quiet.

10. Ice cream and candy _____ sour. They _____ sweet.

◇ **PRACTICE 18. Using IS, ISN'T, ARE, or AREN'T + adjective. (Chart 1-6)**
Directions: Write complete sentences using ***is/isn't*** or ***are/aren't*** and the given words.

1. apples . . . blue / red

   Apples aren't blue. They're red.

2. a circle . . . round / square

   _____

3. a piano . . . heavy / light

   _____

4. potato chips . . . sweet / salty

   _____

5. the Sahara Desert . . . large / small

   _____

6. The Nile River . . . short / long

   _____

7. this exercise . . . easy / difficult

   _____

8. my grammar book . . . new / old

   _____

9. electric cars . . . expensive / cheap

   _____

◇ **PRACTICE 19. Identifying prepositions. (Chart 1-7)**
Directions: Write the preposition in the blank. <u>Underline</u> the prepositional phrase in each sentence.

	PREPOSITION
1. Mike is <u>in his apartment.</u>	*in*
2. Mr. Lee is at the airport.	_____
3. Ali is from Egypt.	_____

4. My book is on my desk. _____

5. Bob's pen is in his pocket. _____

6. The post office is on First Street. _____

7. The post office is next to the bank. _____

8. My feet are under my desk. _____

9. My nose is between my cheeks. _____

10. My apartment is on the third floor. _____

It is above Mr. Kwan's apartment. _____

◇ **PRACTICE 20. Understanding prepositions. (Chart 1-7)**
Directions: Follow the instructions.

Put an "X" . . .

1. above circle A.

2. under circle B.

3. in circle A.

4. between circles A and B.

5. next to circle A.

◇ **PRACTICE 21. Review: nouns, adjectives, and prepositions. (Chart 1-8)**
Directions: Write the words in the correct columns.

✓ *at*	✓ *easy*	*next to*	*single*
between	*empty*	*on*	*sister*
✓ *city*	*happy*	*outside*	*teacher*
country	*hungry*	*parents*	

NOUNS	ADJECTIVES	PREPOSITIONS (OF PLACE)
city	*easy*	*at*
_____	_____	_____
_____	_____	_____
_____	_____	_____
_____	_____	_____

◇ PRACTICE 22. Sentence review. (Chart 1-8)
Directions: Complete the sentences using the given structure.

1. Dr. John Brown is *(noun)* ___a dentist / a doctor, etc.___

   (place) ___here / at home, etc.___

   (adjective) ___friendly / nice, etc.___

2. Anna is *(noun)* _____

   (place) _____

   (adjective) _____

3. Russia is *(adjective)* _____

   (place) _____

   (noun) _____

4. *Basic English Grammar Workbook* is (place) _____

   (adjective) _____

   (noun) _____

◇ PRACTICE 23. Sentence review. (Chart 1-8)
Directions: Make true sentences using the given words and a form of **be**.

1. Canada \ a city

   ___Canada isn't a city.___

2. Canada \ in North America

   _____

3. France \ next to \ Germany

   _____

4. The downstairs of a building \ above \ the upstairs

   _____

5. Ice \ hot

   _____

6. apples and oranges \ vegetables

_____

7. airplanes \ fast

_____

8. alligators \ friendly

_____ alligator

9. an alligator \ dangerous

_____

10. vegetables \ healthy

_____

◇ PRACTICE 24. Review: BE.
Directions: Complete the sentences with the correct form of *be*.

Hiro ___*is*___ from Japan. He _____ a student. Mr. Brown _____ the teacher.
     1   2   3

He _____ very nice. Fifteen students _____ in the class. They _____ friendly.
    4   5   6

Hiro _____ happy in this class.
      7

◇ PRACTICE 25. Review: BE.
Directions: Complete the sentences with the correct form of *be*.

Mrs. Smith: Hi, I ___*am*___ Mrs. Smith. Mr. Brown _____ not here.
                     1   2

            He _____ sick. I _____ your teacher today.
                   3   4

Hiro: Hi, my name _____ Hiro.
                      5

Mrs. Smith: Hi, Hiro. It _____ nice to meet you.
                           6

Hiro: I _____ happy to meet you too.
               7

            This _____ my friend, Mari.
                   8

Mrs. Smith: Hi, Mari. I _____ glad* to meet you too.
                       9

_____

glad = happy

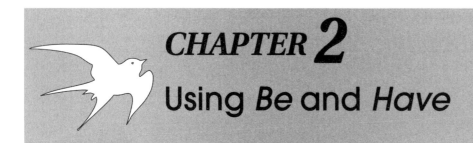

CHAPTER 2
Using *Be* and *Have*

◇ **PRACTICE 1. Yes/no questions with BE. (Chart 2-1)**
Directions: Make yes/no questions with the given words and a form of **be**.

1. you \ a student _____*Are you a student?*_____

2. he \ a student? _____

3. they \ teachers? _____

4. she \ from Canada? _____

5. you \ ready _____

6. we \ ready _____

7. it \ ready _____

◇ **PRACTICE 2. Yes/no questions with BE. (Chart 2-1)**
Directions: Make questions for the given answers.

1. A: _____*Are you a student?*_____
   B: Yes, I am a student.

2. A: _____
   B: Yes, bananas are healthy.

3. A: _____
   B: Yes, Ann is doctor.

4. A: _____
   B: Yes, the children are at school.

5. A: _____
   B: Yes, we are ready for the test.

6. A: _____
   B: Yes, Liz is at school.

7. A: _____
   B: Yes, I am tired.

◇ **PRACTICE 3. Short answers with BE. (Chart 2-2)**
   Directions: Complete the sentences with short answers.

1. Is Paris a city?   Yes, ___*it is*___ .

2. Are Paris and Tokyo cities?   Yes, _____ .

3. Are dogs animals?   Yes, _____ .

4. Is Luis sick today?   Yes, _____ .

5. Are apples fruits?   Yes, _____ .

6. Is the sun hot?   Yes, _____ .

7. Is Pat a woman?   Yes, _____ .

8. Are you a student?   Yes, _____ .

9. Are you students?   Yes, _____ .

10. Am I a student?   Yes, _____ .

◇ **PRACTICE 4. Questions and short answers with BE. (Chart 2-2)**
   Directions: Complete the questions and answers.

| Anna | Mr. Sanchez | Susan | Mrs. Brown | Joe |
| English teacher | English student | photographer | police officer | college student |

1. ___*Is*___ Mr. Sanchez a student? Yes, he ___*is*___ .

2. _____ Anna a teacher? Yes, she _____ .

3. _____ Joe a student? Yes, he _____ .

4. _____ Susan a photographer? Yes, she _____ .

5. _____ Joe and Mr. Sanchez students? Yes, they _____ .

6. _____ Mrs. Brown a police officer? Yes, she _____ .

7. _____ Anna and Susan women? Yes, they _____ .

8. _____ Mr. Sanchez and Joe men? Yes, they _____ .

9. _____ you a student? Yes, I _____ .

10. _____ you and Mr. Sanchez students? Yes, we _____ .

◇ PRACTICE 5. Questions and short answers with BE. (Chart 2-2)
Directions: Make questions and give short answers. Use contractions where possible.

NEW STUDENT INFORMATION	NEW STUDENT INFORMATION
Name: Rosa Gonzalez Country: Spain Age: 22 ___male _X_ female	Name: Dong Vuong Country: Vietnam Age: 24 _X_ male ___female

1. ____*Is*_____ Rosa a student?   Yes, she ____*is*_____ .

2. ____*Is Dong*_____ a student?   Yes, he _____ .

3. _____ students?   Yes, _____ .

4. _____ from Mexico?   No, she _____ .

5. _____ from Vietnam?   Yes, _____ .

6. _____ 22?   Yes, _____ .

7. _____ 25?   No, he _____ .

8. _____ 23?   No, they _____ .

◇ PRACTICE 6. Questions and short answers with BE. (Chart 2-2)
Directions: Complete the conversations. Use contractions where possible.

1. A: ____*Is*____ Elena a student?

   B: Yes, _____*she is*_____ .

   A: _____ a student?

   B: No, I'm not.

2. A: _____ students?

   B: No, we _____ . We _____ teachers.

   A: Is Mr. Ito a teacher?

   B: No, _____ . He _____ a student.

◇ PRACTICE 7. Understanding WHERE. (Chart 2-3)
   Directions: Choose the correct question for each response.

	QUESTION	RESPONSE
1. a.	Where is Tom?	Yes, he is.
(b.)	Is Tom at home?	
2. a.	Are the students in the cafeteria?	They are in the cafeteria.
b.	Where are the students?	
3. a.	Is my grammar book at home?	Yes, it is.
b.	Where is my grammar book?	
4. a.	Where are the dictionaries?	Yes, they are.
b.	Are the dictionaries in the classroom?	
5. a.	Where are you?	I am at home.
b.	Are you at home?	
6. a.	Is the teacher in her office?	She is in her office.
b.	Where is the teacher?	

◇ PRACTICE 8. Questions with BE and WHERE. (Chart 2-3)
   Directions: Make questions.

1. A: ___*Where is the teacher?*___
   B: In the classroom. (The teacher is in the classroom.)

2. A: _____
   B: Yes, she is. (The teacher is in the classroom.)

3. A: _____
   B: At home. (Pablo and Dina are at home.)

4. A: _____
   B: Yes, they are. (Pablo and Dina are at home.)

5. A: _____
   B: Yes, it is. (The map is in the car.)

6. A: _____
   B: On First Avenue. (The store is on First Avenue.)

7. A: _____
   B: Yes, we are. (We are outside.)

8. A: _____
   B: Outside. (We are outside.)

◇ PRACTICE 9. Using HAVE. (Chart 2-4)
  Directions: Create your own chart by completing the sentences with the correct form of **have**.

  1. I   _____ have _____   a book.

  2. You   _____   a book.

  3. She   _____   a book.

  4. He   _____   a book.

  5. Mr. Jones   _____   a book.

  6. The dog   _____   a book.

  7. It   _____   a book.

  8. Mrs. Hill   _____   a book.

  9. They   _____   books.

 10. The students _____   books.

 11. You   _____   books.

◇ PRACTICE 10. BE and HAVE. (Chapter 1 and Chart 2-4)
  Directions: Complete each sentence with the correct form of **be** or **have**.

  My apartment . . .

  1. _____ has _____ five rooms.

  2. _____ is _____ comfortable.

  3. _____ in the city.

  4. _____ twenty years old.

  5. _____ a new kitchen.

  6. _____ expensive.

  7. _____ on the fourth floor.

  8. _____ many windows.

  9. _____ a view of downtown.

  My apartment manager . . .

  1. _____ thirty years old.

  2. _____ brown eyes and brown hair.

  3. _____ tall.

  4. _____ two children.

  5. _____ a small apartment.

  6. _____ friendly.

  7. _____ a student at the university.

  8. _____ very busy.

  9. _____ a busy life.

◇ PRACTICE 11. BE and HAVE. (Chapter 1 and Chart 2-4)
  Directions: Complete the sentences with the correct forms of **be** and **have**.

  1. Several students _____ are _____ absent. They _____ have _____ colds.

  2. Jean _____ a toothache. She _____ at the dentist.

3. I _____ not at school. I _____ a stomachache.

4. My parents _____ sick. They _____ fevers.

5. Mr. Paul _____ a backache. He _____ at home.

◇ PRACTICE 12. BE and HAVE. (Chart 2-4)
Directions: Complete the sentences with **has**, **have**, **is**, or **are**.

The people in Dr. Smith's waiting room ____*are*____ sick. Johnny _____ a

sore throat. Thomas _____ a cold. Mr. and Mrs. White _____ fevers. Mrs.

Martinez _____ a stomachache.

The construction workers _____

backaches. Sara _____ a headache.

Dr. Smith _____ very busy.

◇ PRACTICE 13. Possessive adjectives. (Chart 2-5)
Directions: Complete the sentences. Use **my, your, her, his, our,** or **their**.

1. He has a backpack. _____*His*_____ backpack is heavy.

2. You have a backpack. _____ backpack is heavy.

3. I have a backpack. _____ backpack is heavy.

4. We have backpacks. _____ backpacks are heavy.

5. You have backpacks. _____ backpacks are heavy.

6. They have backpacks. _____ backpacks are heavy.

7. The students have backpacks. _____ backpacks are heavy.

8. Tom has a backpack. _____ backpack is heavy.

9. Kate has a backpack. _____ backpack is heavy.

10. Tom and Kate have backpacks. _____ backpacks are heavy.

11. Kate and I have backpacks. _____ backpacks are heavy.

12. You and I have backpacks. _____ backpacks are heavy.

◇ PRACTICE 14. Possessive adjectives. (Chart 2-5)

Directions: Use the information in the chart to complete the sentences about the after-school activities of Jenny, Bill, Karen, and Kathy. Use **his, her,** or **their.**

Jenny

Bill

Karen

Kathy

Bill

	JENNY	BILL	KAREN AND KATHY
Monday	dance class	soccer practice	baseball game
Tuesday			
Wednesday	piano lesson		soccer practice
Thursday		piano lesson	

1. _____His_____ soccer practice is on Monday.

2. _____ baseball game is on Monday.

3. _____ piano lesson is on Thursday.

4. _____ soccer practice is on Wednesday.

5. _____ piano lesson is on Wednesday.

6. _____ dance class is on Monday.

◇ PRACTICE 15. HAVE and possessive adjectives. (Chart 2-5)
   Directions: Complete the sentences. Use **have** or **has** and **my, your, her, his, our,** or **their**.

   1. I _____*have*_____ a cat. _____*My*_____ cat is friendly.

   2. Peter and Ellen _____ new cell phones. _____ cell phones are small.

   3. You _____ coats. _____ coats are warm.

   4. We _____ an old car. _____ car is slow.

   5. Hector _____ a mustache. _____ mustache is black.

   6. Maria _____ a purse. _____ purse is large.

   7. Thomas _____ a briefcase. _____ briefcase is brown.

   8. Mr. and Mrs. Brown _____ an apartment. _____ apartment is on the top floor.

   9. I _____ a dictionary. _____ dictionary is English-Japanese.

   10. The workers _____ boots. _____ boots are heavy.

◇ PRACTICE 16. THIS/THAT. (Chart 2-6)
   Directions: Complete the sentences with **this** or **that**.

   1. _____*This*_____ is my house key.

   2. _____ is your phone card.

   3. _____ is your checkbook.

   4. _____ is my credit card.

   5. _____ is my briefcase.

   6. _____ is your bag.

7. _____ is your baseball cap.

8. _____ is my wallet.

◇ PRACTICE 17. THESE/THOSE. (Chart 2-7)
Directions: Complete the sentences with **these** or **those**.

1. _____*These*_____ are apples.

2. _____ are oranges.

3. _____ are pears.

4. _____ are lemons.

5. _____ are bananas.

6. _____ are carrots.

◇ PRACTICE 18. THIS, THAT, THESE, and THOSE. (Charts 2-6 and 2-7)
Directions: Complete the sentences with **this**, **that**, **these**, or **those**.

1. *(This, These)* _____*This*_____ book is inexpensive. *(That, Those)* _____*Those*_____ books
   are expensive.

2. *(This, These)* _____ chairs are comfortable. *(That, Those)* _____
   chairs are uncomfortable.

3. *(This, These)* _____ computer is fast. *(That, Those)* _____ computer
   is slow.

4. *(This, These)* _____ cats are friendly. *(That, Those)* _____ cat
   is unfriendly.

5. *(This, These)* _____ cell phone belongs to me. *(That, Those)* _____
   cell phone belongs to Paul.

6. *(This, These)* _____ shoes are comfortable. *(That, Those)* _____ shoes are uncomfortable.

7. *(This, These)* _____ exercise is easy. *(That, Those)* _____ exercises are hard.

◇ **PRACTICE 19. WHO and WHAT. (Chart 2-8)**
Directions: Choose the correct response for each question.

1. Who is that?
   (A.) That is Rita.   B. That is a toy.

2. What is that?
   A. That is an electric car.   B. That is Tom.

3. Who are they?
   A. They are flowers.   B. They are students.

4. What are they?
   A. They are small insects.   B. They are Dick and Mira.

5. Who is this?
   A. This is my new car.   B. This is Kenny.

6. What are they?   batteries (for a watch)
   A. They are my children.   B. They are batteries.

◇ **PRACTICE 20. WHO and WHAT. (Chart 2-8)**
Directions: Make questions with **who** or **what** for the given answers.

1. A: _____*Who is that?*_____
   B: That is the teacher.

2. A: _____
   B: That is an apple.

3. A: _____
   B: Those are digital cameras.

4. A: _____
   B: They are the new students.

5. A: _____
   B: Those are DVDs.

6. A: _____
   B: That is Dr. Benson.

◇ PRACTICE 21. Review: questions and short answers.
  Directions: Answer the questions. Choose from the responses in the list.

Yes, it is.	*This is Donna.*	*Yes, I am.*
It's in Norway.	✓ *Yes, they are.*	*No, it isn't.*
Yes, he is.	*This is an insect.*	*Yes, she is.*

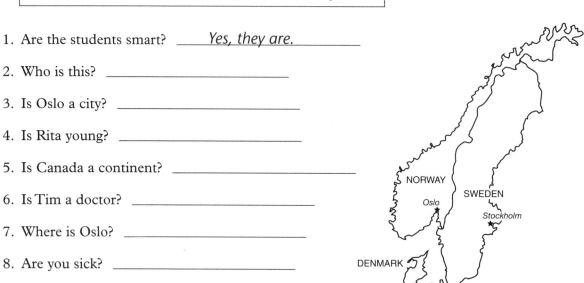

1. Are the students smart? ____*Yes, they are.*____

2. Who is this? _____

3. Is Oslo a city? _____

4. Is Rita young? _____

5. Is Canada a continent? _____

6. Is Tim a doctor? _____

7. Where is Oslo? _____

8. Are you sick? _____

9. What is this? _____

◇ PRACTICE 22. Review: BE and possessive adjectives.
  Directions: Complete the sentences. Use the correct form of **be** and the appropriate possessive adjective.

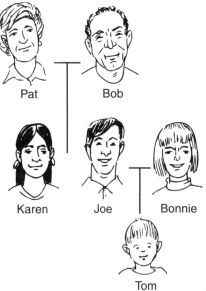

  This is the Jackson family. Pat is the mother. Bob is ___*her*___ husband. They have two
                                                          1

children. _____ children are Karen and Joe. Karen is Joe's sister. Joe is _____
          2   3

brother. Joe and Bonnie are married. They have one child. Tom is _____ son. _____
                                                                 4   5

grandparents are Pat and Bob.

◇ PRACTICE 23. REVIEW: HAVE and BE.

Directions: Complete the sentences with the correct forms of **have** and **be**.

I ___*have*___ one brother and one sister. My brother _____ a nurse. He
      1   2

_____ a good job at a hospital. His name _____ Ronald. He
    3   4

_____ 30 years old. My sister _____ a doctor. She _____ very
    5   6   7

busy. She _____ many patients. Her name _____ Monica. She
          8   9

_____ 35 years old. My name _____ Martha. I _____ 28 years
    10   11   12

old. I _____ an English teacher. We all _____ good jobs. We
      13   14

_____ happy with our work.
    15

CHAPTER 3
Using the Simple Present

◇ **PRACTICE 1. Form of the simple present tense. (Chart 3-1)**

Directions: Create your own chart by completing the sentences with the correct form of **walk**.

1. I ___*walk*___ outside.

2. We _____ outside.

3. They _____ outside.

4. He _____ outside.

5. You _____ outside.

6. She _____ outside.

7. The dog _____ outside.

8. It _____ outside.

9. Mr. and Mrs. Ito _____ outside.

10. Mr. Ito _____ outside.

11. The teacher _____ outside.

12. The students _____ outside.

◇ **PRACTICE 2. The simple present tense. (Chart 3-1)**

Directions: Underline the simple present verbs.

Spiro <u>works</u> at night. He teaches auto mechanics at a school in his town. He leaves his apartment at 5:00. He catches the bus near his home. The bus comes at 5:15. It takes him 40 minutes to get to work. His classes begin at 6:30. He teaches until 10:30. He stays at school until 11:15. A friend drives him home. He gets home around midnight.

◇ **PRACTICE 3. Form of the simple present tense. (Chart 3-1)**
   Directions: Complete the sentences with the correct form of the verb.

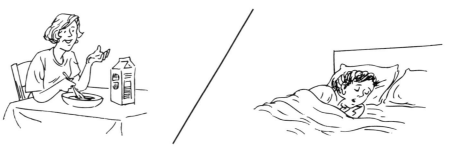

1. My alarm clock *(ring)* _____rings_____ at 5:00 every morning.

2. I *(get)* _____ out of bed slowly.

3. My husband *(make)* _____ breakfast for us.

4. He *(cook)* _____ a hot breakfast every morning.

5. We *(leave)* _____ for work at 6:00.

6. I *(bring)* _____ the newspaper in the car.

7. We *(discuss)* _____ the morning news.

8. My husband and I *(work)* _____ at the same company.

9. We *(arrive)* _____ at work early.

10. Our two co-workers *(come)* _____ later.

11. They *(take)* _____ the same bus to the office.

◇ **PRACTICE 4. Form of the simple present tense. (Chart 3-1)**
   Directions: Complete the sentences with the correct form of the verb.

Joan and I are roommates. We are very different. Joan *(wakes, wake)*

_____wakes_____ up early. I *(wakes, wake)* _____ up at 11:00. I *(eats, eat)*
         1   2

_____ breakfast at lunchtime. Joan *(eats, eat)* _____ breakfast at
        3   4

7:30. She *(leaves, leave)* _____ for school at 8:00. I *(takes, take)*
                                    5

_____ evening classes, so I go to school at 5:00. Joan *(cooks, cook)*
        6

_____ an early dinner and *(falls, fall)* _____ asleep around 9:00.
        7   8

I *(eats, eat)* _____ at midnight and *(falls, fall)* _____ asleep in the
                      9   10

early morning. We *(sees, see)* _____ each other on weekends. We *(has, have)*
                                          11

_____ very different lives, but we are good friends.
        12

◇ **PRACTICE 5. Frequency adverbs. (Chart 3-2)**
Directions: Rewrite each sentence using the given frequency adverb.

1. Olga has cream in her coffee. *(always)*

    Olga always has cream in her coffee.

2. I eat breakfast. *(rarely)*

    _____

3. The students buy their lunch at school. *(seldom)*

    _____

4. They bring a lunch from home. *(usually)*

    _____

5. My husband and I go out to a restaurant for dinner. *(often)*

    _____

6. My husband drinks tea with dinner. *(sometimes)*

    _____

7. We have dessert. *(never)*

    _____

◇ **PRACTICE 6. Frequency adverbs. (Chart 3-2)**
Directions: Rewrite the sentences using an appropriate frequency adverb.

1. Beth has fish for lunch. (50% of the time)

    Beth sometimes has fish for lunch.

2. Roger gets up late. (10% of the time)

    _____

3. Mr. and Mrs. Phillips go to the movies on weekends. (95% of the time)

    _____

4. I clean my apartment. (75% of the time)

_____

5. My roommate cleans our apartment. (0% of the time)

_____

6. The students do their homework. (100% of the time)

_____

7. The teacher corrects papers on weekends. (60% of the time)

_____

◇ PRACTICE 7. Frequency adverbs. (Chart 3-2)
   Directions: Agree or disagree with the sentences about your morning activities. If the answer is *no,* write the correct frequency adverb.

1. I always wake up early.	yes	no
2. I sometimes sleep late on weekends.	yes	no
3. I seldom eat a hot breakfast.	yes	no
4. I often listen to the radio in the morning.	yes	no
5. I usually watch TV during breakfast.	yes	no
6. I rarely study English at home in the morning.	yes	no
7. I never exercise in the morning.	yes	no

◇ PRACTICE 8. Frequency adverbs. (Chart 3-2)
   Directions: Complete these sentences about yourself in the evening.

1. I always _____

2. I never _____

3. I sometimes _____

4. I often _____

5. I seldom _____

6. I rarely _____

◇ PRACTICE 9. Other frequency expressions. (Chart 3-3)
  Directions: Rewrite the sentences using the expressions in the list.

once a day	*once a month*
three times a day	*twice a month*
twice a week	*once a year*
three times a week	*twice a year*

1. I have classes on Mondays, Wednesdays, and Fridays.

   <u>*I have classes three times a week.*</u>

2. I exercise from 10:00 A.M. to 11:00 A.M. every day.

   _____

3. I pay my phone bill on the first day of every month.

   _____

4. I visit my cousins in December and June every year.

   _____

5. Dr. Williams checks her e-mail at 6:00 A.M., noon, and 10:00 P.M. every day.

   _____

6. The Browns take a long vacation in August.

   _____

7. Cyndi gives dinner parties at the beginning and end of each month.

   _____

8. Sam buys vegetables at the farmers' market on Mondays and Fridays.

   _____

◇ PRACTICE 10. Frequency adverbs with BE. (Chart 3-4)
Directions: Complete the sentences with the given frequency adverb.

1. *often*   Joan _____X_____ is _____*often*_____ sick.

2. *often*   Joan _____ feels _____ sick.

3. *sometimes* Carly _____ is _____ hungry.

4. *rarely*   It _____ is _____ cold in the summer.

5. *rarely*   It _____ rains _____ in the summer.

6. *usually*   I _____ am _____ in bed at 9:00.

7. *usually*   I _____ go _____ to bed at 9:00.

8. *never*   I _____ sleep _____ late.

9. *never*   I _____ wake up _____ late.

10. *always*   I _____ am _____ up early.

◇ PRACTICE 11. Frequency adverbs. (Charts 3-2 and 3-4)
Directions: Make sentences using the given words.

1. The teacher \ clean up the classroom \ usually

   _____*The teacher usually cleans up the classroom.*_____

2. The students \ help the teacher \ often

   _____

3. The classroom \ be clean \ always

   _____

4. The parents \ visit the class \ usually

   _____

5. The parents \ help the students with their work \ sometimes

   _____

6. The parents \ be helpful \ always

   _____

◇ PRACTICE 12. Spelling of verbs ending in -S/-ES. (Chart 3-5)
Directions: Write the correct form of the verb in the appropriate column.

✓catch	✓eat	fix	wish	call
finish	talk	sleep	listen	kiss

-S   **-ES**

he _____eats_____   she _____catches_____

he _____   she _____

he _____   she _____

he _____   she _____

he _____   she _____

◇ PRACTICE 13. Final -S/-ES. (Charts 3-1 and 3-5)
Directions: Write the forms for the given verbs.

1. I (teach) _____teach_____ English.

2. She (teach) _____ English.

3. You (mix) _____ the salad.

4. He (mix) _____ the salad.

5. Sara (miss) _____ her friends.

6. They (miss) _____ their friends.

7. I (brush) _____ my hair.

8. The girl (brush) _____ her hair.

9. She and I (wash) _____ the dishes.

10. He (wash) _____ the dishes.

11. He (cook) _____ dinner.

12. She (read) _____ magazines.

13. Richard (watch) _____ movies.

14. Class (begin) _____ early.

15. Many students (come) _____ late.

16. The teacher always (come) _____ on time.

SALAD

◇ **PRACTICE 14. Spelling of verbs ending in -Y. (Chart 3-6)**
Directions: Create your own chart by completing each sentence with the correct form of **study**.

1. The students _____ *study* _____ hard.

2. One student _____ hard.

3. I _____ hard.

4. My friend _____ hard.

5. You _____ hard.

6. We _____ hard.

7. She _____ hard.

8. They _____ hard.

9. He _____ hard.

10. My friends _____ hard.

◇ **PRACTICE 15. Spelling of verbs ending in -Y. (Chart 3-6)**
Directions: Write the correct form of each verb in the appropriate column.

✓*pay*	✓*try*	*worry*	*play*	*say*
buy	*enjoy*	*fly*	*cry*	*study*

-IES

he _____ *tries* _____

he _____

he _____

he _____

he _____

-S

she _____ *pays* _____

she _____

she _____

she _____

she _____

Review: simple present tense. (Charts 3-5 and 3-6)

Directions: Complete each sentence with the correct form of verb in the list. You may use a verb more than one time.

fly	*close*	*study*	*fix*	*start*
call	*brush*	*stop*	*help*	

1. Dr. Lee _____*starts*_____ work at 6:00 every day.

2. Sara _____ her teeth after every meal.

3. The grocery store _____ at 11:00 every night.

4. Birds _____ south in the winter.

5. An airplane often _____ over my house.

6. I'm lucky. The bus _____ in front of my apartment building.

7. Martha is a mechanic. She _____ cars.

8. I talk to my mother on the phone every day. I _____ her, or she

   _____ me.

9. Inga _____ in the library every afternoon.

10. John is a teacher's assistant. He _____ the teacher with her work.

◇ PRACTICE 17. **Irregular singular verbs: HAS, DOES, and GOES.** (Chart 3-7)

Directions: Make sentences about the people in the chart. Use the correct form of **have class at, do homework at,** and **go to work at.**

	JIMI	MARTA	SUSAN	PAUL
9:00	class		homework	homework
10:00	homework	class		
11:00	work	homework	class	class
1:00			work	work
2:00		work		

1. Jimi

   a. He _____*has class at 9:00.*_____

   b. He _____

   c. He _____

2. Marta

    a. She _____

    b. She _____

    c. She _____

3. Susan and Paul

    a. They _____

    b. They _____

    c. They _____

◇ **PRACTICE 18. Review: simple present tense.** (Charts 3-5 → 3-7)
    Directions: Complete the sentences with the words in parentheses.

        Ricardo *(leave)* _____*leaves*_____ his house at 4:30 every morning. He *(catch)*
                      1

_____ the bus near his house. He *(get)* _____ to work at 5:00. He *(work)*
      2   3

_____ in a restaurant. He *(fix)* _____ wonderful dishes from his country.
    4   5

Many people *(come)* _____ to the restaurant for his food. He *(finish)*
                  6

_____ work at 3:00. Then he *(meet, often)* _____ with
    7   8

students from his country and *(help)* _____ them with English. They *(have, usually)*
                            9

_____ dinner together. After dinner he *(go)* _____ home.
    10   11

Sometimes he *(have)* _____ a snack. He *(be)* _____ tired at the end of the day, but
              12   13

he *(enjoy)* _____ his work and the time with the students from his country.
        14

CHART 3-A: REVIEW OF FINAL -S PRONUNCIATION: VOICELESS AND VOICED SOUNDS

VOICELESS	VOICED	

(a) /p/ sleep
   /t/ write
   /f/ laugh
	(b) /b/ rub
	   /d/ ride
	   /v/ drive
		Some sounds are "voiceless." You don't use your voice box. You push air through your teeth and lips. For example, the sound /p/ comes from air through your lips. The final sounds in (a) are voiceless.

		Some sounds are "voiced." You use your voice box to make voiced sounds. For example, the sound /b/ comes from your voice box. The final sounds in (b) are voiced.

(c) sleeps = *sleep*/s/
    writes = *write*/s/
    laughs = *laugh*/s/
	(d) rubs = *rub*/z/
	    rides = *ride*/z/
	    drives = *drive*/z/
		Final **-s** is pronounced /s/ after voiceless sounds, as in (c). Final **-s** is pronounced /z/ after voiced sounds, as in (d).

I can feel my voice box. It vibrates.

◇ PRACTICE 19. Final -S pronunciation: voiceless sounds. (Charts 3-8 and 3-A)
Directions: The final sounds of the verbs in these sentences are "voiceless." Final **-s** is pronounced /s/.

PART A. Read the sentences aloud.

1. Mike **sleeps** for eight hours every night.
    sleep/s/

2. Our teacher always **helps** us.
    help/s/

3. Jack **writes** a letter to his girlfriend every day.
    write/s/

4. Sara never **laughs**.
    laugh/s/

5. Sue usually **drinks** a cup of coffee in the morning.
    drink/s/

6. Kate **walks** to school every day.
    walk/s/

PART B. Underline the verb in each sentence. Pronounce it. Then read the sentence aloud.

7. My child often <u>claps</u> her hands.

8. Olga always bites her pencil in class.

9. Maria usually gets up at seven-thirty.

10. Yoko asks a lot of questions in class.

11. Ahmed always talks in class.

12. Sue coughs when she is nervous.

◇ **PRACTICE 20. Final -S pronunciation: voiced sounds. (Charts 3-8 and 3-A)**
Directions: The final sounds of the verbs in these sentences are "voiced." Final *-s* is pronounced /z/.

PART A. Read the sentences aloud.

1. Cindy **rides** the bus to school.
   ride/z/

2. Jack usually **drives** his car to school.
   drives/z/

3. Rain **falls**.
   fall/z/

4. Sally often **dreams** about her boyfriend.
   dream/z/

5. Sometimes Jim **runs** to class.
   run/z/

6. Tina **wears** blue jeans every day.
   wear/z/

7. Ann always **sees** Mr. Lee at the market.
   see/z/

PART B. Underline the verb in each sentence. Pronounce it. Then read the sentence aloud.

8. The teacher often <u>stands</u> in the front of the room.

9. George lives in the dormitory.

10. Jean rarely smiles.

11. Sam always comes to class on time.

12. It rains a lot in London.

13. Jack always remembers his wife's birthday.

14. It snows in New York City in the winter.

◇ **PRACTICE 21. Final -ES spelling and pronunciation. (Charts 3-8 and 3-A)**
Directions: Which verbs are pronounced /əz/ in the third-person singular? Write those verbs below with the correct form for *he*.

✓brush	hate	leave	fix	miss	kiss
love	catch	stay	invite	teach	take

he . . .

1. _____brushes_____   4. _____

2. _____   5. _____

3. _____   6. _____

◇ PRACTICE 22. Final -ES spelling and pronunciation. (Charts 3-8 and 3-A)
Directions: Add the correct ending: **-s** or **-es**. Then circle the correct pronunciation. Practice pronouncing the words.

1. Alice fix _es_ cars. /s/ /z/ (/əz/)

2. Rob like _____ chocolate. /s/ /z/ /əz/

3. Donna sleep _____ late. /s/ /z/ /əz/

4. Nate run _____ fast. /s/ /z/ /əz/

5. My mother write _____ stories. /s/ /z/ /əz/

6. The baby wear _____ diapers. /s/ /z/ /əz/

7. Our teacher think _____ a lot. /s/ /z/ /əz/

8. Pat drive _____ a sports car. /s/ /z/ /əz/

9. The student miss _____ his parents. /s/ /z/ /əz/

10. Ms. Kim help _____ her students. /s/ /z/ /əz/

◇ PRACTICE 23. The simple present tense and review of BE: negative. (Charts 1-5 and 3-9)
Directions: Write the correct form of the verb. Use the negative.

	HAVE	*EAT*	*BE*
1. I	_don't have_	_____	_am not_
2. You	_____	_____	_____
3. He	_____	_doesn't eat_	_____
4. She	_____	_____	_____
5. It	_____	_____	_____
6. We	_____	_____	_aren't_
7. They	_____	_____	_____

◇ PRACTICE 24. The simple present tense: negative. (Chart 3-9)
Directions: Rewrite the sentences using the negative form.

1. I have time. _I don't have time._

2. You need more time. _____

3. They eat breakfast. _____

4. Yoshi likes bananas. _____

5. Susan does her homework. _____

6. We walk to school. _____

7. The phone works. _____

◇ **PRACTICE 25. The simple present tense: negative. (Chart 3-9)**
   Directions. Use the given words to make true sentences.

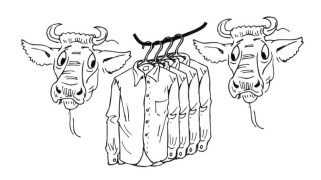

1. *wear*   Cows _____ *don't wear* _____ shirts.

2. *be*   Fruit _____ *is* _____ healthy.

3. *have*   A child _____ gray hair.

4. *break*   Glass _____.

5. *grow*   Apples _____ on grass.

6. *walk*   A newborn baby _____.

7. *fly*   Cars _____.

8. *have*   People _____ twenty fingers.

9. *help*   A doctor _____ sick people.

10. *fix*   A dentist _____ broken legs.

11. *fix*   A dentist _____ broken teeth.

12. *like*   Mice _____ cats.

13. *chase*   Cats _____ mice.

◇ PRACTICE 26. The simple present tense: negative. (Chart 3-9)

Directions: Use the information to make true sentences about Tom, Janet, and Mark.

	TOM	JANET	MARK
drink coffee	x	x	
watch TV			x
walk to school	x		
study grammar	x	x	x
go shopping		x	
take the bus		x	x
skip lunch	x	x	
eat dinner at home	x		x
eat dinner out★		x	

★*eat dinner out* = eat dinner at a restaurant.

PART A. What do Tom, Janet, or Mark do every day? Write sentences using the given words.

1. *(drink coffee)* _____Tom and Janet drink coffee._____

2. *(watch TV)* _____

3. *(walk to school)* _____

4. *(study grammar)* _____

5. *(go shopping)* _____

PART B. What don't Tom, Janet, or Mark do every day? Write sentences using the given words.

6. *(take the bus)* _____Tom doesn't take the bus._____

7. *(watch TV)* _____

8. *(skip lunch)* _____

9. *(eat dinner at home)* _____

10. *(eat dinner out)* _____

◇ **PRACTICE 27. The simple present tense: negative. (Chart 3-9)**

Directions: Complete the sentences. Use the words in parentheses. Use the simple present tense.

1. Alex *(like)* _____*likes*_____ tea, but he *(like, not)* _____*doesn't like*_____ coffee.

2. Sara *(know)* _____ Ali, but she *(know, not)* _____ Hiroshi.

3. Pablo and Maria *(want)* _____ to stay home tonight. They *(want, not)* _____ to go to a movie.

4. Robert *(be, not)* _____ hungry. He *(want, not)* _____ _____ a sandwich.

5. Mr. Smith *(drink, not)* _____ coffee, but Mr. Jones *(drink)* _____ twelve cups every day.

6. I *(be, not)* _____ rich. I *(have, not)* _____ a lot of money.

7. This pen *(belong, not)* _____ to me. It *(belong)* _____ to Pierre.

8. My friends *(live, not)* _____ in the dorm. They *(have)* _____ an apartment.

9. It *(be)* _____ a nice day today. It *(be, not)* _____ cold. You *(need, not)* _____ your coat.

10. Today *(be)* _____ a holiday. We *(have, not)* _____ class today.

11. Abby *(eat, not)* _____ breakfast. She *(be, not)* _____ hungry in the mornings.

12. I *(read)* _____ the newspaper. I *(watch, not)* _____ TV news.

13. My roommate *(read, not)* _____ the newspaper. She *(watch)* _____ TV news.

◇ PRACTICE 28. Yes/no questions. (Chart 3-10)
   Directions: Make questions with the given words.

   1. she \ study _____*Does she study?*_____

   2. they \ study _____

   3. he \ know _____

   4. the doctor \ know _____

   5. we \ know _____

   6. I \ understand _____

   7. you \ understand _____

   8. the students \ understand _____

   9. your roommate \ work _____

  10. the car \ work _____

  11. it \ work _____

  12. I \ work _____

◇ PRACTICE 29. Yes/no questions. (Chart 3-10)
   Directions: Below is information about four people and the exercise they get. Make
   questions for the given answers.

	TOM	ROGER	RENEE	LISA
swim	x			
run		x		
play soccer	x		x	x
lift weights		x		

   1. Tom

      a. _____*Does he swim?*_____ Yes, he does.

      b. _____ Yes, he does.

      c. _____*Does he run?*_____ No, he doesn't.

      d. _____ No, he doesn't.

2. Roger

    a. _____ Yes, he does.

    b. _____ No, he doesn't

    c. _____ Yes, he does.

3. Renee and Lisa

    a. _____ Yes, they do.

    b. _____ No, they don't.

    c. _____ No, they don't

◇ PRACTICE 30. Short answers to yes/no questions. (Chart 3-10)
Directions: Choose the correct response for each question.

1. Do you like fish?
   (A.) Yes, I do.   B. Yes, I like.

2. Does your husband like fish?
   A. Yes, he does.   B. Yes, he likes.

3. Do you want to go out to dinner?
   A. Yes, I want.   B. Yes, I do.

4. Do you have a question?
   A. Yes, I have.   B. Yes, I do.

5. Do you need help?
   A. Yes, I do.   B. Yes, I need.

6. Does your friend need help?
   A. Yes, she needs.   B. Yes, she does.

7. Do your friends go to school?
   A. Yes, they do.   B. Yes, they go.

8. Does your husband teach English?
   A. Yes, he teaches.   B. Yes, he does.

◇ PRACTICE 31. Yes/no questions and answers. (Chart 3-10)
Directions: Make questions. Give short answers.

1. Ann is a doctor. She examines children.

      Does she examine adults?   No,   *she doesn't.*

2. Tom is a mechanic. He fixes cars.

   _____ boats? No, _____.

3. I am a pilot. I fly small planes.

_____ jets?   No, _____.

4. We are teachers. We teach teenagers.

_____ young children? No, _____.

5. Lynn and Doug are architects. They design houses.

_____ offices? No, _____.

6. My sister and I are janitors. We clean office buildings.

_____ schools? No, _____.

7. Mrs. Adams is a writer. She is a writer for a magazine.

_____ for a book company? No, _____.

8. I am a nurse. I am a nurse at a hospital. _____

at a clinic? No, _____.

9. They are construction workers. They are construction workers for a hotel.

_____ for an office building?

No, _____.

10. Dr. Smith is a musician. He is musician for a symphony.

_____ for a rock band?

No, _____.

◇ PRACTICE 32. Questions with WHERE. (Chart 3-11)
Directions: Check (✓) the sentences that answer the question *where*.

1. __✓__ Gino lives in Rome.

2. _____ Thomas is a doctor.

3. _____ Thomas works at Valley Hospital.

4. _____ Mr. and Mrs. Rogers have five children.

5. _____ The children like to play soccer.

6. _____ The children like to play at the park.

7. _____ Helene goes to Tahiti for vacation.

8. _____ I need a vacation.

◇ **PRACTICE 33. Questions with WHERE. (Chart 3-11)**
Directions: Read the story. Make **where**-questions about Paulo for the given answers.

Paulo has an interesting work life. He spends most of his time outdoors. He has two jobs, one for the summer and one for the winter. In the summer, he works in the forest. He watches for forest fires. He stays in a lookout tower. In the winter, he works in the mountains. He is a ski instructor. He teaches young children how to ski. He lives in a small ski hut with other teachers. Paulo loves his work. He is happy to be outdoors.

lookout tower

ski hut

1. A: _____*Where does Paulo spend most of his time?*_____

   B: Outdoors.

2. A: _____

   B: In the forest.

3. A: _____

   B: In a lookout tower.

4. A: _____

   B: In the mountains.

5. A: _____

   B: In a small ski hut.

◇ **PRACTICE 34. Questions with WHERE. (Chart 3-11)**
Directions: Make questions for the given answers.

1. A: _____*Where does David live?*_____

   B: In Miami. (David lives in Miami.)

2. A: _____

   B: In the classroom. (The teacher is in the classroom.)

3. A: _____

   B: At the Plaza Hotel. (Dr. Varma stays at the Plaza Hotel.)

4. A: _____

   B: Yes, she does. (She stays at the Plaza Hotel.)

5. A: _____

   B: On First Street. (I catch the bus on First Street.)

6. A: _____

   B: Yes, I do. (I catch the bus on First Street.)

7. A: _____

   B: In the park. (The construction workers eat lunch in the park.)

8. A: _____

   B: No, she isn't. (My mother isn't outside.)

9. A: _____

   B: Downstairs. (She is downstairs.)

◇ PRACTICE 35. WHEN and WHERE in questions. (Chart 3-12)
   Directions: Complete the questions with **when** or **where**.

   1. ____*Where*____ does Tom work?   At the bank.

   2. ____*When*____ does he leave for work?   At 7:00.

   3. _____ does he eat lunch?   At noon.

   4. _____ does he eat?   At his desk.

   5. _____ does he go after work?   To the gym.

   6. _____ does he go home?   At 8:00.

   7. _____ does he eat dinner?   In front of the TV.

   8. _____ does he have dinner?   At 9:00.

   9. _____ does he get ready for bed? After dinner.

   10. _____ does he sleep?   On his sofa.

◇ PRACTICE 36. Review: yes/no and *wh*-questions. (Charts 3-10 → 3-12)
   Directions: Make questions for the given answers.

   1. A: ____*When do you go to bed?*____
      B: Around 10:00. (I go to bed around 10:00.)

   2. A: _____
      B: Yes, I do. (I get up early.)

   3. A: _____
      B: At 6:30. (The bus comes at 6:30.)

   4. A: _____
      B: Yes, it does. (The bus comes on time.)

   5. A: _____
      B: At a hospital. (I work at a hospital.)

   6. A: _____
      B: At 7:00. (I start work at 7:00.)

   7. A: _____
      B: At 4:00. (I leave work at 4:00)

8. A: _____

  B: Yes, I do. (I like my job.)

9. A: _____

  B: Yes, it is. (It is interesting work.)

◇ PRACTICE 37. Review: yes/no and *wh*-questions. (Charts 3-10 → 3-12)
  Directions: Read the note. Then make questions and answers about Dr. Ramos and his schedule.

  1. be \ a science teacher?

    _____*Is he a teacher?*_____

    _____*Yes, he is.*_____

  2. what \ teach?

    _____

    _____

  3. where \ teach \ chemistry?

    _____

    _____

  4. when \ be \ in the chemistry lab?

    _____

    _____

  5. where \ teach \ biology?

    _____

    _____

  6. be \ in his office \ every day?

    _____

    _____

  7. be \ in his office \ at 1:00?

    _____

    _____

  8. teach \ at 8:00?

    _____

    _____

  9. when \ teach?

    _____

    _____

Dr. Ramos

Schedule Change

My new office hours
are from 1:00 to
2:00, Monday,
Wednesday, and
Friday. I teach
biology at 9:00
and 10:00 in the
biology lab. I teach
chemistry at 12:00
in the chemistry lab.

◇ PRACTICE 38. BE and DO in questions. (Chart 3-13)
   Directions: Complete the questions with a form of **be** or **do**.

   1. _____*Are*_____ you ready for the bus?
   2. _____ the bus here?
   3. _____ the bus usually come on time?
   4. _____ you often ride the bus?
   5. _____ the bus ride short?
   6. _____ you do your work on the bus?
   7. _____ you read books on the bus?
   8. _____ you enjoy the ride?
   9. _____ you drive to work sometimes?
   10. _____ you tired of my questions?

◇ PRACTICE 39. BE and DO in questions. (Chart 3-13)
   Directions: Complete the questions and answers. Use a form of **be** or **do**.

   1. A: _____*Are*_____ you sick?
      B: No, I _____ not.
      A: _____ you tired?
      B: Yes, I _____.
      A: _____*Do*_____ you want to go to bed?
      B: No, I _____.

   2. A: _____ you know the time?
      B: Yes, I _____. It _____ 5:55.

   3. A: _____ you hungry?
      B: Yes, I _____.
      A: _____ you want some chocolate.
      B: Sure. Mmmm.
      A: _____ you like it?
      B: No, I _____. I love it!!

   4. A: _____ you students?
      B: Not exactly.
      A: _____ you teachers?
      B: Not exactly.
      A: What _____ you?
      B: We _____ student teachers.

5. A: _____ Mr. Jones here?

   B: No, he _____ .

   A: Where _____ he?

   B: I have no idea.

   A: _____ his wife here?

   B: No, she _____ .

   A: Where _____ she?

   B: With Mr. Jones.

6. A: Where _____ my glasses? _____ you know?

   B: No. _____ they in your purse?

   A: No, they _____ .

   B: _____ they in your pocket?

   A: No.

   B: Oh, I see them! They _____ on your head.

◇ **PRACTICE 40. Chapter review: simple present tense.**

Directions: Complete the sentences with the correct form of the verb. Some sentences are negative, and some are not.

1. Mario likes to talk. He *(be)* _____*isn't*_____ quiet.

2. Janna isn't quiet. She *(love)* _____*loves*_____ to talk.

3. Susan is a good student. She *(study)* _____ a lot.

4. The nurses are very busy. They *(have)* _____ time for long lunches.

5. John's bedroom is messy. He *(clean)* _____ it often.

6. This soup is delicious. It *(taste)* _____ wonderful.

7. A new car is expensive. It *(cost)* _____ a lot of money.

8. Several students want to answer the question. They *(know)* _____ the answer.

9. Several students don't know the answer. They *(want)* _____ to answer the question.

10. A: Your eyes are red. You *(look)* _____ tired.

    B: Actually, I'm sad. I *(be)* _____ tired.

◇ **PRACTICE 41. Question review. (Chapters 2 and 3)**
Directions: Make questions using the information in the note.

fridge = refrigerator.

1. A: _____*Is Jane at home?*_____

   B: No, she isn't. (Jane isn't home.)

2. A: _____

   B: At work. (She is at work.)

3. A: _____

   B: No, they aren't. (Susie and Johnny aren't home.)

4. A: _____

   B: At school. (They are at school.)

5. A: _____

   B: At 6:00. (Dinner is at 6:00.)

6. A: _____

   B: A pizza. (Jane has a pizza in the fridge.)

◇ **PRACTICE 42. Review: simple present tense.**
Directions: Add *-s/-es* or Ø (nothing) where necessary.

Sam enjoy __*s*__ cooking. He often make _____ new recipes. He and his wife
         1   2

like _____ to have company for dinner. They invite _____ me to dinner once a month.
    3   4

When I arrive, I go _____ to the kitchen and watch _____ him cook. He usually has three
             5   6

or four pots on the stove. He watch _____ the pots carefully. He make _____ a big mess
                           7   8

in the kitchen. After dinner, he always wash _____ all the dishes and clean _____ the
                                              9   10
kitchen. His wife never cook _____ for us. She know _____ Sam is a much better cook.
                             11   12

◇ PRACTICE 43. Chapter review: simple present tense.
    Directions: Choose the correct completion for each sentence.

    1. Alex _____ know French.
        A. isn't   (B.) doesn't   C. don't

    2. _____ Alex speak Russian?
        A. Is   B. Does   C. Do

    3. _____ Alex from Canada?
        A. Is   B. Does   C. Do

    4. When _____ you usually study?
        A. are   B. does   C. do

    5. Anita _____ a job.
        A. no have   B. no has   C. doesn't have

    6. Omar _____ his new car every Saturday.
        A. wash   B. washs   C. washes

    7. Where does Tina _____ to school?
        A. go   B. goes   C. to go

    8. Fumiko _____ English at this school.
        A. study   B. studies   C. studys

    9. Fumiko and Omar _____ students at this school.
        A. is   B. are   C. be

    10. They _____ speak the same language.
        A. aren't   B. doesn't   C. don't

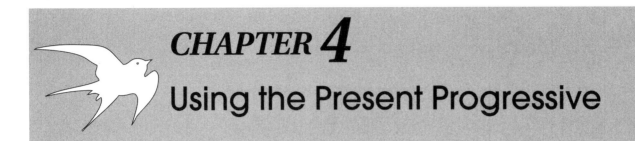

CHAPTER 4
Using the Present Progressive

◇ **PRACTICE 1. The present progressive. (Chart 4-1)**
Directions: Complete the sentences with **am**, **is**, or **are**.

RIGHT NOW

1. Some students ___are___ waiting for the bus.

2. Their teacher _____ correcting their homework.

3. I _____ doing my homework.

4. Mark _____ doing his homework.

5. Sandra _____ shopping at the mall.

6. Her friends _____ shopping with her.

7. Dr. John _____ looking for medical information on the Internet.

8. A nurse _____ talking to a patient.

9. Several patients _____ waiting in the waiting room.

10. Mr. and Mrs. Brown _____ watching TV.

11. Their daughter _____ reading a book.

12. You _____ reading this exercise.

13. We _____ learning English.

14. My friend and I _____ learning English.

◇ **PRACTICE 2. Spelling of -ING. (Chart 4-2)**
Directions: Write the **-ing** forms for the verbs.

1. shine ___shining___

2. win _____

3. join _____

4. sign _____

5. fly _____

6. pay _____

7. study _____

8. get _____

9. wait _____

10. write _____

◇ **PRACTICE 3. Spelling of -ING.** (Chart 4-2)

Directions: Write the **-ing** forms for the verbs.

1. dream _____dreaming_____   7. hurt _____

2. come _____   8. clap _____

3. look _____   9. keep _____

4. take _____   10. camp _____

5. bite _____

6. hit _____

◇ **PRACTICE 4. The present progressive.** (Charts 4-1 and 4-2)

Directions: Complete the sentences with the correct form of the verbs in the list. Use the present progressive.

come	go	read	talk
do	kick	sit	✓wait

It's 3:00 and the classroom is empty. Some students are outside. They _____are waiting_____
                                                                          1

for the city bus. A few students _____ on the ground under a tree.
                                              2

They _____ about their plans for the weekend. A girl on a bench
              3

_____ her homework. The boy next to her _____ a book.
        4   5

A few students _____ a soccer ball. The bus _____ now.
                        6   7

The students _____ home.
                    8

◇ PRACTICE 5. The present progressive. (Chart 4-3)
   Directions: Make sentences for each part of this practice.

PART A. Tony is an engineer. Right now he is in his office. Check (✓) the activities he is doing. Make possible sentences for all the given phrases.

    __✓__ meet with his manager   _____ talk on the phone

    _____ repair his car   _____ ride a horse

    _____ work at his computer   _____ buy food for dinner

1.   *He is meeting with his manager.*

2.   *He isn't repairing his car.*

3. _____

4. _____

5. _____

6. _____

PART B. Anita and Ben are nurses. Right now they are at the hospital. Check (✓) the activities they are doing. Make possible sentences for all the given phrases.

    _____ talk to patients   _____ work with doctors

    _____ wash cars   _____ give medicine to patients

    _____ watch movies

1. _____

2. _____

3. _____

4. _____

5. _____

PART C. What are you doing right now? Check (✓) the activities and make possible sentences for all the given phrases.

    _____ listen to music   _____ study in the library

    _____ sit at a desk   _____ wait for a friend

    _____ work at home   _____ ride on a bus

1. _____

2. _____

3. _____

4. _____

5. _____

6. _____

◇ **PRACTICE 6. The present progressive: negative. (Chart 4-3)**
   Directions: Use the verbs in the sentences to make true sentences.

   1. I *(think)* ____am thinking / am not thinking____ about my family right now.

   2. I *(write)* _____ in a classroom right now.

   3. I *(go)* _____ to the airport today.

   4. I *(travel)* _____ to another country today.

   5. A cat *(sit)* _____ beside me right now.

   6. A bird *(sing)* _____ outside my window.

   7. My phone *(ring)* _____ at this moment.

   8. A computer near me *(make)* _____ noise right now.

◇ **PRACTICE 7. The present progressive: questions. (Chart 4-4)**
   Directions: Make questions with the given words. Use the present progressive.

   1. he \ study English? ____*Is he studying English?*____

   2. you \ work? _____

   3. they \ leave? _____

   4. she \ stay home? _____

   5. we \ going to school? _____

   6. the computer \ work? _____

   7. it \ work? _____

   8. I \ drive? _____

   9. your friend \ come? _____

   10. the students \ laugh? _____

   11. Mr. Kim \ sleep? _____

   12. Monica \ dream? _____

◇ PRACTICE 8. The present progressive: questions and negatives. (Chart 4-4)

Directions: Use the information in *italics* to make logical questions and answers.

1. Anna is in the kitchen. *(sleep, cook)*

   A: _____*Is she sleeping*_____?

   B: No, ____*she isn't*____. She ____*is cooking*____.

2. Pablo is in the car. *(drive, run)*

   A: _____?

   B: No, _____. He _____.

3. Terry and Tony are in the swimming pool. *(swim, study)*

   A: _____?

   B: No, _____. They _____.

4. Mrs. Ramirez is at the supermarket. *(teach, shop)*

   A: _____?

   B: No, _____. She _____.

5. The Smiths are in the mountains. *(clean, hike)*

   A: _____?

   B: No, _____. They _____.

6. Marta is in her bedroom. *(sleep, fish)*

   A: _____?

   B: No, _____. She _____.

7. The children are in the park. *(play, work)*

   A: _____?

   B: No, _____. They _____.

8. I am on a plane. *(ride a bike, sit)*

   A: _____?

   B: No, _____. I _____.

◇ **PRACTICE 9. Simple present vs. the present progressive. (Chart 4-5)**
   Directions: Choose the correct completion for each sentence.

   1. I send e-mails   now.   (every day.)
   2. I am not sending an e-mail   (now.)   every day.
   3. I receive e-mails   now.   every day.
   4. I look at magazines   now.   every day.
   5. I'm reading a book   now.   every day.
   6. It's raining   now.   every day.
   7. My dog plays outside   now.   every day.
   8. My dog and cat are playing outside   now.   every day.
   9. My computer isn't working   now.   every day.
   10. I work at my computer   now.   every day.

◇ **PRACTICE 10. Simple present vs. the present progressive. (Chart 4-5)**
   Directions: Check (✓) the sentences that describe activities happening right now.

   1. __✓__ The phone is ringing.   6. _____ The baby is crying.
   2. _____ I'm talking to my sister.   7. _____ She cries when she is hungry.
   3. _____ We talk two or three times a week. 8. _____ Her mother is feeding her.
   4. _____ Ruth exercises in the mornings.   9. _____ We are listening to music.
   5. _____ She lifts weights.   10. _____ We listen to music in the car.

◇ **PRACTICE 11. Simple present vs. the present progressive. (Chart 4-5)**
   Directions: Complete the sentences with the correct form of the verbs in *italics*.

   Right now the sun *(shine)* _____*is shining*_____ . I *(look)*

   _____₂_____ out my window at the lake. A man and young boy *(fish)*

   _____₃_____ from a small boat. A mother with a baby *(sit)*

   _____₄_____ on the grass. They *(play)* _____₅_____ with a

   ball. Two girls *(swim)* _____₆_____ near the shore. Some teenage boys *(jump)*

   _____₇_____ off the dock.

I (swim) _____ in the lake every day in the summer for exercise.
                    8

In the winter, I usually (walk) _____ around the lake, or I (go)
                                          9

_____ to a gym.
        10

Today I (work) _____ at home. I usually (work)
                        11

_____ at home three days a week. I (write)
        12

_____ stories for children's books. Right now,
        13

I (write) _____ a story about a young boy and girl and a magic hat.
                    14

◇ PRACTICE 12. Simple present vs. the present progressive. (Chart 4-5)
   Directions: Complete the sentences with ***Do***, ***Does***, ***Is***, or ***Are***.

   1. _____*Do*_____ you study every day?

   2. _____ you working hard now?

   3. _____ your class working hard now?

   4. _____ you learning a lot of English?

   5. _____ you memorize vocabulary every day?

   6. _____ your teacher helping you now?

   7. _____ your teacher help you after class?

   8. _____ you do your homework every day?

   9. _____ the homework take a long time?

   10. _____ you understand your classmates?

   11. _____ your teacher understand you?

   12. _____ you ask a lot of questions?

   13. _____ you studying with friends right now?

   14. _____ you often study with friends?

◇ PRACTICE 13. Nonaction verbs. (Chart 4-6)
   Directions: Choose the correct verb form in each sentence.

   1. (*Do you know,*) *Are you knowing* the names of all the students in your class?

   2. Mmm. I *smell, am smelling* something good in the oven.

   3. The baby *cries, is crying* right now. She *is wanting, wants* her mother.

   4. This coffee *is tasting, tastes* wonderful. I *like, am liking* strong coffee.

   5. The cat and dog *are running, run* outside right now. The dog *likes, is liking* the cat,

      but the cat *is hating, hates* the dog.

◇ **PRACTICE 14. Nonaction verbs. (Chart 4-6)**
Directions: Complete each sentence with the correct form of the verb in *italics*.

1. A: Mmm. This bread *(taste)* _____*tastes*_____ delicious.

   B: Thank you. I *(think)* _____ it has honey in it.

2. A: What *(Jan, want)* _____ for her birthday?

   B: Well, she *(need)* _____ a winter coat, but she *(want)*

   _____ leather boots.

3. A: Shhh. *(you, hear)* _____ a siren?

   B: I *(hear)* _____ it, but I *(see, not)*

   _____ it.

4. A: Jackie *(love)* _____ Carl.

   B: What? I *(believe, not)* _____ you. Carl *(love)*

   _____ me!

◇ **PRACTICE 15. SEE, LOOK AT, WATCH, HEAR, and LISTEN TO. (Chart 4-7)**
Directions: Choose the correct sentence in each pair.

1. a. I am hearing the neighbor's TV. It's very loud.
   (b.) I hear the neighbor's TV. It's very loud.

2. a. Look! I see a mouse on the road.
   b. Look! I am seeing a mouse on the road.

3. a. Annette isn't listening to me right now.
   b. Annette doesn't listen to me right now.

4. a. Shhh. I'm watching a movie.
   b. Shhh. I watch a movie.

5. a. I look at the clock. We are late.
   b. I'm looking at the clock. We are late.

6. a. Mary, what are you looking at?
   b. Mary, what do you look at?

7. a. Do you hear that noise? It sounds like an earthquake.
   b. Are you hearing that noise? It sounds like an earthquake.

8. a. I am listening to the radio at night. It helps me fall asleep.
   b. I listen to the radio at night. It helps me fall asleep.

9. a. I hear my cell phone. I need to answer it right now.
   b. I am hearing my cell phone. I need to answer it right now.

◇ **PRACTICE 16. SEE, LOOK AT, WATCH, HEAR, and LISTEN TO. (Chart 4-7)**
Directions: Complete the sentences with the verb in parentheses.

Andy is sitting in his living room right now. He

(watch) ____*is watching*____ a football game on TV. His
 1

favorite team *(play)* _____. He
 2

(listen, also) _____ to the game
 3

on the radio and *(look)* _____
 4

at sports information in the newspaper. He *(wear)*

_____ headphones. His
 5

wife *(talk)* _____ to him. She *(tell)*
 6

_____ him her plans for the day. He *(listen, not)*
 7

_____ because he *(hear, not)* _____
 8 9

her. Suddenly, she turns off the TV. Now Andy *(listen)* _____
 10

very carefully.

◇ **PRACTICE 17. SEE, LOOK AT, WATCH, HEAR, and LISTEN TO. (Chart 4-7)**
Directions: Choose the correct verb in each sentence.

1. In the evenings, I like to sit in front of the TV and (*watch,*) *see* old movies.

2. The neighbors are having a party. I *hear, listen to* a lot of loud noise.

3. Shhh. I *hear, listen to* something. Is someone outside?

4. I love rock music. When I'm at home, I turn on the stereo, sit down, and *hear, listen to* rock music.

5. A: Let's go shopping. I want to *look at, watch* clothes.

   B: Okay. You can *look at, see* clothes. I want to sit on a bench and *see, watch* the people at the mall.

6. A: Look out the window. *Do you see, Do you watch* the storm clouds?

   B: I *see, look at* several dark rain clouds.

◇ **PRACTICE 18. Review. (Charts 4-6 and 4-7)**
Directions: Write true sentences using the given verbs.

Right now I . . .

1. *(look at)* _____ .

2. *(see)* _____ .

3. *(hear)* _____.

4. *(listen to)* _____.

5. *(watch)* _____.

6. *(want)* _____.

7. *(need)* _____.

◇ PRACTICE 19. THINK ABOUT / THINK THAT. (Chart 4-8)
Directions: Choose the correct sentence in each pair.

1. a. You are very quiet. What do you think about?
   b. You are very quiet. What are you thinking about?

2. a. I am thinking about my plans for today.
   b. I think about my plans for today.

3. a. I am thinking that grammar is difficult.
   b. I think that grammar is difficult.

4. a. What do you think? Does this shirt look okay?
   b. What are you thinking? Does this shirt look okay?

5. a. Joe, do you think that sports stars get too much money?
   b. Joe, are you thinking that sports stars get too much money?

◇ PRACTICE 20. THINK ABOUT / THINK THAT. (CHART 4-8)
Directions: Complete the sentences with the correct form of ***think*** or ***think about***.

1. A: What _____*are*_____ you _____*thinking about*_____
      right now?

   B: I _____ my family. I miss them.

   A: You have a nice family. I _____ you are lucky.

2. A: Some people _____ English is an easy language.

   B: I _____ not _____

      it is easy to learn. I _____ it is difficult.

3. A: I have a new game. I _____ an animal. It
      is very long and sometimes dangerous. Do you know the animal? Can you guess?

   B: _____ you _____ a snake?

   A: Yes!

   B: I _____ snakes make nice pets, but many people are
      afraid of them.

   A: I'm afraid of them. I _____ they are scary.

◇ PRACTICE 21. Verb review. (Chapters 3 and 4)

    Directions: Complete each sentence with the correct form of the verb in *italics*.

1. Tony's family *(eat)* _____eats_____ dinner at the same time every day.

   During dinner, the phone sometime *(ring)* _____.

   Tony's mother *(answer, not)* _____ it. She *(want, not)*

   _____ the children to talk on the phone during dinner. She

   (believe) _____ dinner is an important time for the family.

2. Olga Burns is a pilot for an airline company in Alaska. She *(fly)* _____

   almost every day. Today she *(fly)* _____ from Juneau to
   Anchorage.

3. A: Hello?

   B: Hello. This is Chris. Is Pam there?

   A: Yes, but she can't come to the phone right now. She *(take)* _____
   a shower. Can she call you back in about ten minutes?

   B: Sure. Thanks. Bye.

   A: Bye.

4. A: Excuse me. *(you, wait)* _____ for the downtown bus?

   B: Yes, I *(be)* _____. Can I help you?

   A: Yes. What time *(the bus, stop)* _____ here?

   B: Ten thirty-five.

   A: *(be, usually, it)* _____ on time?

   B: Yes. It *(come, rarely)* _____ late.

5. A: What *(your teacher, do, usually)* _____
   at lunchtime every day?

   B: I *(think)* _____ she *(correct)* _____

   papers in the classroom and *(have)* _____ lunch.

   A: What *(she, do)* _____ right now?

   B: She *(talk)* _____ to a student.

6. A: *(you, know)* _____ the capital of Australia?

   B: I *(believe)* _____ it *(be)* _____ Vienna.

   A: Not Austria. Australia!

   B: Oh. Wait a minute. Let me think. I *(know)* _____. It's
   Canberra.

CHAPTER 5
Talking About the Present

◇ **PRACTICE 1. Using IT with time and dates. (Chart 5-1)**

Directions: Read the e-mail message. Make questions for the answers. Begin each question with ***What***.

> To: Jim
> Date: March 5, 2006
>
> Hi Jim,
>
> It's 6:00 Monday morning in Tokyo. I'm sitting in my hotel room. I'm waiting for the airport bus. Great trip—I'll tell you about it tomorrow. Don't forget to pick me up!
>
> Miss you,
> Sue

1. _____*What day is it?*_____ It's Monday.

2. _____ It's 6:00 A.M.

3. _____ It's March 5th.

4. _____ It's 2006.

5. _____ It's March.

6. _____ It's six o'clock.

7. _____ It's the 5th of March.

◇ **PRACTICE 2. Using IT with time and dates. (Chart 5-1)**

Directions: Choose the correct response to each question.

1. What's the date today?
   (A.) It's April 1.   B. It's Monday.

2. What day is it?
   A. It's February 2.   B. It's Friday.

3. What month is it?

   A. It's January 2nd.   B. It's December.

4. What time is it?

   A. It's 9:55.   B. It's 9:55 o'clock.

5. What's the date today?

   A. It's Monday.   B. It's the 2nd of May.

◇ **PRACTICE 3. Prepositions of time. (Chart 5-2)**

   Directions: Complete each sentence with the correct preposition.

   1. I wake up . . .

      a. ___*in*___ the morning.

      b. _____ 7:00.

   2. My husband goes to work . . .

      a. _____ 1:00 P.M.

      b. _____ the afternoon.

      c. _____ Mondays, Wednesdays, and Thursdays.

   3. I work . . .

      a. _____ the evening.

      b. _____ night.

      c. _____ 5:00 _____ midnight.

      d. _____ 5:00.

      e. _____ Saturday.

      f. _____ Saturdays.

   4. My husband was born . . .

      a. _____ December.

      b. _____ December 26.

      c. _____ the afternoon.

      d. _____ 1:00 _____ the afternoon.

      e. _____ December 26, 1980.

      f. _____ 1980.

◇ PRACTICE 4. Prepositions of time. (Chart 5-2)

Directions: Complete the sentences with *in*, *on*, *at*, *from*, or *to*.

1. I have English class ____*in*____ the morning.

2. My first class begins _____ 9:00 A.M.

3. The class goes _____ 9:00 _____ 9:55.

4. I don't have class _____ Fridays.

5. My math class meets _____ the evenings.

6. I don't like to study _____ night.

7. I prefer to study _____ the afternoon.

8. There is no class _____ May 1st.

9. Summer vacation goes _____ June _____ September.

◇ PRACTICE 5. Talking about the weather. (Chart 5-3)

Directions: Use the weather information in the list.

Moscow	0°C	32°F	partly cloudy, snow
Sydney	24°C	75°F	clear, dry
Seoul	5°C	40°F	heavy rain, strong winds
Cairo	38°C	100°F	clear, dry

PART A. Make questions for the given answers.

1. _____ *How's the weather/What's the weather like in Cairo?* _____ It's hot.

2. _____ It's warm.

3. _____ It's stormy.

4. _____ It's beautiful.

5. _____ It's freezing.

PART B. Circle *yes* or *no*.

6. It is chilly in Moscow.   (yes)   no

7. It is wet in Cairo.   yes   no

8. It is freezing in Seoul.   yes   no

9. It is humid in Sydney.   yes   no

10. It is nice in Sydney.   yes   no

11. It is clear in Seoul.   yes   no

◇ PRACTICE 6. Question review: time and weather. (Charts 5-1 and 5-3)
   Directions: Choose the correct completion for each sentence.

   1. What _____ the weather like today?
      A. is it   (B.) is

   2. What month _____?
      A. is it   B. is

   3. What _____ the date today?
      A. is it   B. is

   4. What day _____?
      A. is it   B. is

   5. What time _____?
      A. is it   B. is

   6. How _____ the weather?
      A. is it   B. is

   7. What year _____?
      A. is it   B. is

◇ PRACTICE 7. THERE + BE. (Chart 5-4)
   Directions: Look around the room you are in. Choose the correct verb and then circle **yes** or **no**.

   1. There (*is,*) *are* one student in this room.   yes   no

   2. There *is, are* two students in this room.   yes   no

   3. There *is, are* a desk.   yes   no

   4. There *is, are* one door.   yes   no

   5. There *is, are* two doors.   yes   no

   6. There *is, are* three windows.   yes   no

   7. There *is, are* a computer.   yes   no

   8. There *is, are* a TV.   yes   no

   9. There *is, are* chairs.   yes   no

◇ **PRACTICE 8. THERE + BE. (Chart 5-4)**
   Directions: Make sentences about the picture using the given words.

1. *(two chairs)* <u>There are two chairs.</u>

2. *(one sofa)* _____

3. *(one table)* _____

4. *(four books)* _____

5. *(one lamp)* _____

6. *(two pillows)* _____

◇ **PRACTICE 9. THERE + BE: yes/no questions. (Chart 5-5)**
   Directions: Think about your bedroom. Circle the correct form of *be*. Then write short
   answers.

1. (*Is,*) *Are*   there a bed in your bedroom?   <u>Yes, there is. / No, there isn't.</u>

2. *Is,* *Are*   there a window in your bedroom?   _____

3. *Is,* *Are*   there four windows in your bedroom?   _____

4. *Is,* *Are*   there a pillow on your bed?   _____

5. *Is,* *Are*   there six pillows on your bed?   _____

6. *Is,* *Are*   there sheets on your bed?   _____

7. *Is,* *Are*   there a TV in your bedroom?   _____

8. *Is,* *Are*   there two closets in your bedroom?   _____

9. *Is,* *Are*   there a mirror in your bedroom?   _____

◇ PRACTICE 10. THERE + BE: yes/no questions. (Chart 5-5)
Directions: You are new to a town. Make questions about the places in parentheses. Begin with **Is there** or **Are there**.

1. *(a subway)* _____Is there a subway?_____

2. *(a bus station)* _____

3. *(fast-food restaurants)* _____

4. *(movie theaters)* _____

5. *(a park)* _____

6. *(places to go running)* _____

7. *(a visitor information office)* _____

◇ PRACTICE 11. THERE + BE: questions with HOW MANY. (Chart 5-6)
Directions: Choose the correct noun in each question.

1. How many *boy,* (*boys*) are there in the world?

2. How many *girl, girls* are there in the world?

3. How many *car, cars* are there in the world?

4. How many *word, words* are there in a dictionary?

5. How many *minute, minutes* are there in a day?

6. How many *second, seconds* are there in a day?

7. How many *star, stars* are there in the sky?

8. How many *snowflake, snowflakes* are there in a snowball?

    Directions: Complete the questions with the words from the box. Begin with ***How many.***

colors	countries	main languages
✓continents	letters	states

1.   <u>How many continents are there</u> in the world? There are seven.

2.   _____ in Australia? There are six.

3.   _____ on the Thai flag? There are three.

4.   _____ in Great Britain? There are three.

5.   _____ in the English alphabet? There are twenty-six.

6.   _____ in Canada? There are two: French and English.

◇ PRACTICE 13. THERE + BE: questions with HOW MANY. (Chart 5-6)
    Directions: Make questions using the given words and ***How many.*** Then give short answers.

1. sentence \ in this exercise

   <u>How many sentences are there in this exercise?</u>   <u>There are seven.</u>

2. exercise \ in this chapter

   _____   _____

3. page \ in your dictionary

   _____   _____

4. student \ in your class

   _____   _____

5. male \ in your class

   _____   _____

6. female \ in your class

   _____   _____

7. teacher \ at your school

   _____   _____

◇ PRACTICE 14. Prepositions of place. (Chart 5-7)
　　Directions: Complete the sentences with the correct preposition: **in, on,** or **at**.

　　1. Marco lives _____*in*_____ Italy.

　　2. Tina lives _____ Vancouver, Canada.

　　3. Tina works _____ Burrard Avenue.

　　4. Margaret lives _____ 6456 1st Street.

　　5. Margaret lives _____ 1st Street.

　　6. Jeffrey lives _____ Australia.

　　7. Jeffrey works _____ 2nd Street.

　　8. Jeffrey works _____ 5725 2nd Street.

◇ PRACTICE 15. Prepositions of place. (Chart 5-8)
　　Directions: Complete the sentences with a preposition. There may be more than one possible completion.

　　1. The rabbit is _____*in / inside*_____ the hat.

　　2. The rabbit is _____ the hat.

　　3. The rabbit is _____ the hat.

　　4. The rabbit is _____ the hat.

　　5. The rabbit is _____ the hat.

6. The rabbit is _____ the hat.

7. The rabbit is _____ the hat.

8. The rabbit is _____ the hats.

◇ PRACTICE 16. Prepositions of place. (Charts 5-7 and 5-8)
    Directions: Answer the questions with prepositional expressions.

1. Where are your legs?

    Under my desk. / On the floor. / Etc.

2. Where are your feet?

    _____

3. Where is your left hand?

    _____

4. Where is your right hand?

    _____

5. Where is your workbook?

    _____

6. Where is your pen or pencil?

    _____

◇ PRACTICE 17. NEED/WANT (Chart 5-9)

Directions: Think about what most people ***need*** for life in the twenty-first century and what many people ***want*** to have. Write the words in the list in the correct column.

✓ air	a DVD player	food	a place to live
a camera phone	electricity	a leather coat	a sports car
diamond jewelry	an expensive house	money	water

NEED

air
_____
_____
_____
_____
_____

WANT

_____
_____
_____
_____
_____

◇ PRACTICE 18. NEED/WANT + noun or infinitive. (Chart 5-9)

Directions: Add ***to*** where necessary. Add **Ø** if ***to*** is not necessary.

1. The students need ___to___ finish their art projects.

2. They want ___Ø___ more time.

3. They want _____ an extra week.

4. They need _____ do more work in their free time.

5. Their teacher wants them _____ work hard.

6. She wants _____ their best work.

7. Their teacher wants _____ see their best work.

8. The students want _____ good grades.

◇ PRACTICE 19. NEED/WANT + noun or infinitive. (Chart 5-9)
Directions: Write sentences with the given words.

  1. the children \ need \ a snack

   _____*The children need a snack.*_____

  2. they \ want \ have \ potato chips and soda

   _____

junk food

  3. their mother \ want \ give \ them \ apples and oranges

   _____

  4. the children \ want, not \ eat \ fruit

   _____

  5. they \ want \ junk food

   _____

  6. they \ need \ eat \ healthy food

   _____

Salad

healthy food

◇ PRACTICE 20. WOULD LIKE. (Chart 5-10)
Directions: Create your own chart by completing the sentences with the correct form of
would like.

  1. I   _____*would like*_____   to leave.

  2. You   _____   to leave.

  3. He   _____   to leave.

  4. She   _____   to leave.

  5. The cat   _____   to leave.

  6. Mrs. Jones   _____   to leave.

  7. We   _____   to leave.

  8. They   _____   to leave.

  9. The students _____   to leave.

 10. Their teacher _____   to leave.

 11. My friend   _____   to leave.

 12. My parents   _____   to leave.

◇ PRACTICE 21. WOULD LIKE vs. LIKE.   (Chart 5-11)
   Directions: Decide the meaning of each sentence. Choose **want** or **like**.

   1. I would like a cup of coffee.   (want)   like

   2. I enjoy coffee in the morning.   want   like

   3. My husband enjoys tea.   wants   likes

   4. He would like to try decaffeinated tea.   wants   likes

   5. I don't enjoy decaffeinated coffee.   want   like

   6. We would like some coffee now.   want   like

◇ PRACTICE 22. WOULD LIKE vs. LIKE.   (Chart 5-11)
   Directions: Rewrite the sentences. Use **would like** where possible.

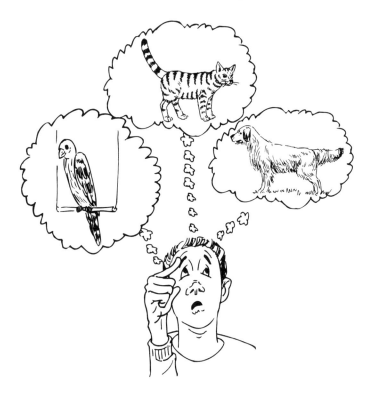

   1. Mark wants to have a large family. ____*Mark would like to have a large family.*____

   2. He enjoys children. ____*(no change)*_____

   3. Children enjoy John. _____

   4. Mark wants to get married this year. _____

   5. He wants a pet this year, too. _____

   6. He enjoys cats, dogs, and birds. _____

   7. What does he want first? _____

◇ PRACTICE 23. Chapter review.

Directions: Choose the correct completion for each sentence.

1. There _____ in our classroom.
   A. is twenty desks   (B.) are twenty desks   C. is twenty desk   D. are twenty desk

2. What _____ today?
   A. day is it   B. is day   C. day it   D. is it day

3. How many _____ there in your class?
   A. students are   B. student is   C. students   D. student

4. Dr. Smith is tired. She _____ to go home and sleep now.
   A. likes   B. would likes   C. would like   D. like

5. There _____ in a minute.
   A. is sixty second   B. are sixty second   C. is sixty seconds   D. are sixty seconds

6. The students _____ finish their work.
   A. needs to   B. need   C. needs   D. need to

7. What _____ the weather like in Bangkok?
   A. is   B. does   C. do   D. are

8. José likes to sit _____ the room.
   A. in middle of   B. in the middle of   C. middle of   D. in middle

9. How _____ in Tokyo?
   A. the weather   B. is the weather C. weather   D. is weather

10. Pam works _____ Broadway Avenue.
    A. next   B. at   C. in   D. on

CHAPTER 6
Nouns and Pronouns

◇ **PRACTICE 1. Identifying nouns. (Chart 6-1)**

Directions: Check (✓) the words that are nouns. Remember, nouns are *persons*, *places*, or *things*.

1. __✓__ father
2. _____ happy
3. _____ play
4. _____ young
5. _____ cats
6. _____ radio
7. _____ Beijing
8. _____ Mary
9. _____ hospital
10. _____ eat

◇ **PRACTICE 2. Identifying nouns. (Chart 6-1)**

Directions: Read the message. <u>Underline</u> the nouns.

*cell = cell phone.

◇ PRACTICE 3. Identifying subjects. (Chart 6-1)
Directions: <u>Underline</u> the subjects.

1. <u>The weather</u> is very cold today.

2. Snow is falling.

3. The sun isn't shining.

4. The children and their parents are playing outside in the snow.

5. Some people are throwing snowballs.

6. Teenagers are building huge snowmen.

◇ PRACTICE 4. Identifying objects. (Chart 6-1)
Directions: Read the sentences and answer the questions. Then write the object. Remember, objects come after the verb and answer the question ***What?*** or ***Who?***

OBJECT

1. Birds eat worms. What do birds eat? _____*Worms.*_____   _____*worms*_____

2. Fish live in the sea. Can you answer "what" or "who?" _____*No.*_____   _____*Ø*_____

3. Doctors help patients. Who do doctors help? _____   _____

4. Babies drink milk. What do babies drink? _____   _____

5. Babies drink several times a day.
   Can you answer "who" or "what?" _____   _____

6. Babies watch their mothers carefully.
   Who do babies watch? _____   _____

◇ PRACTICE 5. Identifying objects. (Chart 6-1)
Directions: Check (✓) the sentences that have objects of verbs. <u>Underline</u> the objects.

1. a. __✓__   I read the <u>newspaper</u>.
   b. _____   I read every morning.
   c. __✓__   I read the <u>newspaper</u> every morning.

2. a. _____   The children play every day.
   b. _____   The children play at the park.
   c. _____   The children play soccer.

3. a. _____ My father cooks several times a week.

   b. _____ My father cooks eggs.

   c. _____ My father cooks eggs several times a week.

4. a. _____ Dogs chew bones.

   b. _____ Dogs chew furniture.

   c. _____ Dogs chew with their sharp teeth.

bone

5. a. _____ We are eating.

   b. _____ We are eating lunch.

6. a. _____ Jan teaches English.

   b. _____ Jan teaches at a private college.

   c. _____ Jan teaches three days a week.

   d. _____ Jan teaches English three days a week.

7. a. _____ Joe is staying with his cousins.

   b. _____ Joe is staying with his cousins for one week.

8. a. _____ Pedro helps with the housework.

   b. _____ Pedro helps Maria with the housework.

◇ PRACTICE 6. Prepositions. (Chart 6-1)

Directions: Check (✓) the prepositional phrases. Then <u>underline</u> the noun that is the object of each preposition. Remember, prepositions are words like *in*, *on*, *at*, *from*, *to*, *with*, *by*, etc.

1. _____ every day

2. __✓__ in the <u>morning</u>

3. _____ with her children

4. _____ on the table

5. _____ is paying money

6. _____ some trees and flowers

7. _____ across the street

8. _____ three times a week

9. _____ at work

10. _____ near my house

◇ PRACTICE 7. Identifying objects of prepositions. (Chart 6-1)

Directions: Check (✓) the sentences that have objects of prepositions. <u>Underline</u> the objects.

1. a. __✓__ Samira works at a <u>bakery</u>.

   b. _____ Samira works very hard.

2. a. _____ I have chocolate in my backpack.

   b. _____ I have chocolate a few times a week.

   c. _____ I have chocolate for a snack.

3. a. _____ Jake and Monica study together.

   b. _____ Jake and Monica study in the library.

   c. _____ Jake and Monica study every evening.

   d. _____ Jake and Monica study at night.

4. a. _____ The teacher is speaking with her students.

   b. _____ The teacher is speaking quickly.

   c. _____ The teacher is speaking in the classroom.

◇ PRACTICE 8. Identifying nouns and adjectives. (Chart 6-2)
   Directions: Write the words from the list in the correct column.

nervous

✓*fresh*	✓*food*	*leg*	*easy*	*test*
poor	*car*	*bright*	*tree*	*rain*
nervous	*chair*	*quiet*	*wet*	

NOUNS   ADJECTIVES

_____ food _____   _____ fresh _____

_____   _____

_____   _____

_____   _____

_____   _____

_____   _____

_____   _____

◇ PRACTICE 9. Nouns and adjectives. (Chart 6-2)
   Directions: Write the adjective that has the opposite meaning.

1. happy   _____ sad _____

2. new   _____

3. soft   _____

4. beautiful   _____

5. young   _____

6. boring   _____

7. fast   _____

8. tall   _____

9. easy   _____

10. noisy   _____

◇ PRACTICE 10. Identifying nouns and adjectives. (Chart 6-2)
Directions: Write "N" over the nouns and "A" over the adjectives.

           N   A   N
1. My sister lives in a new apartment.

2. It is very bright.

3. The rooms are large and have tall ceilings.

4. Her building is next to a Japanese restaurant.

5. I love food from other countries.

6. Mexican food is spicy and delicious.

7. There is a wonderful cafe in my neighborhood.

8. My neighbors like to meet there for coffee.

◇ PRACTICE 11. Using adjectives. (Chart 6-2)
Directions: Choose two to four adjectives to describe the given nouns. Adjectives may be used more than once. Use Chart 6-2, p. 161, in the student book for ideas.

1. _____ _smart,_ _____ students

2. _____ tests

3. _____ neighbors

4. _____ fruit

◇ PRACTICE 12. Adjectives. (Chart 6-2)
Directions: Listed are some nationality adjectives. Write the country next to each adjective.

NATIONALITY	COUNTRY
1. American	_the United States (America)_
2. Australian	_____
3. Canadian	_____

	NATIONALITY	COUNTRY
4.	Chinese	_____
5.	Egyptian	_____
6.	Indian	_____
7.	Indonesian	_____
8.	Italian	_____
9.	Japanese	_____
10.	Korean	_____
11.	Malaysian	_____
12.	Mexican	_____
13.	Russian	_____
14.	Saudi Arabian	_____

Write two more:

_____   _____

_____   _____

◇ PRACTICE 13. Using adjectives. (Chart 6-2)
Directions: Answer the questions. Use nationality adjectives in your answers.

1. What are your favorite ethnic foods? (Ethnic food is food from another country.)

   _____

2. What kind of foreign films (movies from other countries) do you enjoy?

   _____

3. What cultures do you know something about?

   _____

◇ PRACTICE 14. Subject and object pronouns. (Chart 6-3)
Directions: Complete the sentences. Use pronouns (*I*, *me*, *he*, *him*, etc.). Remember, object pronouns come after the verb and answer *Who?* or *What?*

1. Susan knows Thomas. _____*She*_____ knows _____*him*_____ well.

2. Thomas knows Susan. _____ knows _____ well.

3. Susan helps her co-workers. _____ helps _____ a lot.

4. Thomas helps his co-workers. _____ helps _____ a lot.

5. Susan and Thomas help their co-workers. _____ help _____ a lot.

6. Thomas and Susan often see Mr. Jones. _____ don't know _____ well.

7. Thomas and Susan often see Mrs. Jones. _____ don't know _____ well.

8. Susan and Thomas don't talk to their neighbors very much. _____ don't know

_____ well.

9. The neighbors don't talk to Susan and Thomas very much. _____ don't know

_____ well.

◇ **PRACTICE 15. Subject and object pronouns. (Chart 6-3)**
   Directions: Complete each sentence with the correct subject or object pronoun.

1. Grandpa John is in the picture. Do you see _____*him*_____?

2. Grandma Ella is in the picture. Do you see _____?

3. My son and daughter are in the picture. Do you see _____?

4. Your brother is in the picture. Do you see _____?

5. I am in the picture. Do you see _____?

6. Your brother and I are in the picture. Do you see _____?

7. King, our dog, is in the picture. Do you see _____?

8. Queen, our cat, is in the picture. Do you see _____?

9. I don't see your sister. Where is _____*she*_____?

10. I don't see King. Where is _____?

11. I don't see the dog and cat. Where are _____?

12. I don't see my son. Where is _____?

13. I don't see my brother and you. Where are _____?

14. I don't see you. Where are _____?

◇ PRACTICE 16. Object pronouns. (Chart 6-3)
Directions: Complete each sentence with the correct pronoun (***her, him, it, them***).

1. A: When do you take your children to school?
   B: I take _____*them*_____ at 8:30.

2. A: When do you have breakfast?
   B: I have _____ at 9:00.

3. A: When do you call your friends?
   B: I call _____ between breakfast and lunch.

4. A: When do you call your husband?
   B: I call _____ during lunch.

5. A: When do you visit your parents?
   B: I visit _____ on weekends.

6. A: When do you check your e-mail messages?
   B: I check _____ when I wake up.

7. A: When do you listen to the radio.
   B: I listen to _____ in the car.

8. A: When do you talk to your teacher, Mrs. Davis?
   B: I talk to _____ after class.

9: A: When do you see Mr. Gomez?
   B: I see _____ in class.

◇ PRACTICE 17. Object pronouns. (Chart 6-3)
Directions: Choose the correct response for each question.

1. Where do you buy organic apples?
   A. I buy at the farmers' market.   (B.) I buy them at the farmers' market.

2. When do you see the manager, Mr. Owens?
   A. I see him on Mondays.   B. I see on Mondays.

3. When do you get your newspaper?
   A. I get in the evenings.   B. I get it in the evenings.

4. Where do you watch TV?
   A. I watch in the living room.   B. I watch it in the living room.

5. What time do you set your alarm clock for?
   A. I set it for 7:00 A.M.   B. I set for 7:00 A.M.

◇ PRACTICE 18. Subject and object pronouns. (Chart 6-3)
Directions: Use pronouns to complete the sentences.

1. A: How are Mr. and Mrs. Carson?

   B: _____*They*_____ are fine. _____ are taking care of their

   grandchildren right now. They enjoy taking care of _____*them*_____.

2. A: Do you know Nathan and Vince?

   B: Yes, I do. _____ are in my chemistry class. I sit behind

   _____. _____ help me with my homework. The class

   is really hard, and I don't always understand _____.

3. A: That's Ms. Williams. Do you know _____?

   B: Yes, I do. _____ is the kindergarten teacher. The children love

   _____.

4. A: Would you like to join Paul and me for dinner this evening?

   B: Yes, _____ would. Thank you. Can I bring something? Do you want

   _____ to bring a salad?

   A: No, thanks. Paul is cooking, and _____ has everything he needs.

◇ PRACTICE 19. Review: subject and object pronouns and possessive adjectives.
          (Charts 2-5 and 6-3)
Directions: Review the information. Complete the sentences.

SUBJECT PRONOUNS	POSSESSIVE ADJECTIVES	OBJECT PRONOUNS
I	*my*	*me*
you	*your*	*you*
she	*her*	*her*
he	*his*	*him*
it	*its*	*it*
we	*our*	*us*
they	*their*	*them*

1. I have a book. _____*My*_____ book is red. Please give it to _____*me*_____.
2. You have a book. _____*Your*_____ book is red. I'm giving it to _____.
3. She has a book. _____ book is red. Please give it to _____.
4. He has a book. _____ book is red. Please give it to _____.
5. We have books. _____ books are red. Please give them to _____.
6. They have books. _____ books are red. Please give them to _____.

7. I have a female cat. _____ fur is black. I like to play with _____.

8. I have a male cat. _____ fur is brown. I like to play with _____.

9. My new car is blue. _____ seats are red. I love driving _____.

◇ PRACTICE 20. Review: subject and object pronouns and possessive adjectives.
        (Charts 2-5 and 6-3)
Directions: Complete the sentences with the correct words.

1. Hi. (*I, My, Me*) _____My_____ name is Kathy. How are you?

2. This isn't my textbook. It doesn't belong to (*I, my, me*) _____.

3. Where is Jon? I don't see (*he, his, him*) _____. I don't see

    (*he, his, him*) _____ bike.

4. Your dress is beautiful. Is (*it, its, she*) _____ new?

5. Do (*you, your, you're*) _____ have a map? We are lost.

6. We have two young children. (*We, Our, Us*) _____ son is three, and

    (*we, our, us*) _____ daughter is five.

7. This fruit isn't good. (*It, Its, It's*) _____ skin is brown.

8. Dogs like to hide (*it, their, them*) _____ bones.

◇ PRACTICE 21. Review: subject and object pronouns and possessive adjectives.
        (Charts 2-5 and 6-3)
Directions: Complete the sentences with the correct words.

1. Frederick is an artist. (*He, His, Him*) _____He_____

    draws cartoons. (*He, His, Him*) _____ cartoons

    are very funny. I like to watch (*he, his, him*) _____
    when he draws.

2. The children are doing (*they, them, their*) _____ homework.

    (*They, Them, Their*) _____ are working hard. Sometimes I help

    (*they, them, their*) _____ with (*they, them, their*) _____
    homework.

3. Mary is a surgeon. (*She, Her*) _____ works long hours. (*She, Her*)

    _____ family doesn't see (*she, her*) _____ very much.

4. Mr. and Mrs. Cook are on vacation. I am taking care of *(they, them, their)*

_____ dog and cat. *(They, Them, Their)* _____

dog likes to play, but *(they, them, their)* _____ cat likes to sleep.

5. My husband and *(I, me, my)* _____ own a restaurant together. We

enjoy *(we, our, us)* _____ work. Sometimes *(we, our, us)*

_____ friends and family help *(we, our, us)* _____

at the restaurant.

◇ PRACTICE 22. Singular and plural nouns. (Chart 6-4)
Directions: Complete the lists with the correct forms of the given nouns.

	SINGULAR	PLURAL
1.	box	boxes
2.	tomato	_____
3.	zoo	_____
4.	_____	pens
5.	baby	_____
6.	key	_____
7.	_____	cities
8.	_____	wives
9.	dish	_____
10.	thief	_____

◇ PRACTICE 23. Singular and plural nouns. (Chart 6-4)
Directions: Write the plural form of the noun under the correct column.

lady	✓ girl	party	✓ wife	tray	life	city	coin
glass	potato	bush	baby	tax	shoe	leaf	thief

-S	*-IES*	*-VES*	*-ES*
girls	_____	wives	_____
_____	_____	_____	_____
_____	_____	_____	_____
_____	_____	_____	_____

◇ **PRACTICE 24. Pronunciation of noun endings. (Chart 6-4)**
Directions: Write each word in the list under the correct pronunciation ending.

boys	cups	places
wishes	seas	papers
✓ hats	books	faces

/s/	/z/	/əz/
hats	_____	_____
_____	_____	_____
_____	_____	_____

◇ **PRACTICE 25. Spelling and pronunciation of nouns. (Chart 6-4)**
Directions: Complete each sentence with the plural form of the noun in *italics*. Then circle the correct pronunciation for the plural ending.

1. *(Potato)* _____Potatoes_____ are my favorite vegetable.   /s/ (/z/) /əz/

2. Where are the car *(key)* _____?   /s/ /z/ /əz/

3. My English *(class)* _____ meet in the afternoon.   /s/ /z/ /əz/

4. The police want to catch the car *(thief)* _____ soon.   /s/ /z/ /əz/

5. The students are studying for their *(test)* _____.   /s/ /z/ /əz/

6. *(Baby)* _____ don't like loud noises.   /s/ /z/ /əz/

7. I need two *(box)* _____ for these gifts.   /s/ /z/ /əz/

8. Why does Richard have four *(radio)* _____ in his kitchen?   /s/ /z/ /əz/

9. During the holidays, we go to many *(party)* _____.   /s/ /z/ /əz/

10. Miriam has ten *(cat)* _____ in her apartment.   /s/ /z/ /əz/

11. The *(match)* _____ are wet. They don't work.   /s/ /z/ /əz/

12. How many *(textbook)* _____ do you need for your English class?   /s/ /z/ /əz/

13. I like *(dictionary)* _____ with easy definitions.   /s/ /z/ /əz/

14. Do you think cats have nine *(life)* _____? /s/ /z/ /əz/

15. Before you cook carrots, you need to cut off   /s/ /z/ /əz/

    the *(top)* _____.

16. The wind is blowing the *(leaf)*

    _____ off the trees.   /s/ /z/ /əz/

17. I usually have *(sandwich)* _____ for   /s/ /z/ /əz/

    lunch.

◇ PRACTICE 26. Irregular plural nouns. (Chart 6-5)
    Directions: Complete the sentences with the plural form of the appropriate noun.

child	foot	mouse	✓tooth
fish	man	sheep	woman

lamb

1. A dentist fixes _____teeth_____.

2. Cats like to catch _____.

3. Baby lambs become _____.

4. There are many different kinds of _____ in the sea.

5. We put shoes on our _____.

6. In your culture, do _____ and women have the same freedoms?

7. Some movies are very violent. They are not good for _____.

8. Are men and _____ very different?

◇ PRACTICE 27. Review: complete/incomplete sentences.
    Directions: Check (✓) the incorrect sentences and correct them.

              work
1. __✓__ I ∧ in my home office in the morning.

2. ____ My parents work at a university.

3. ____ My father in the library.

4. ____ Is a teacher.

5. _____ My mother a professor.

6. _____ Is an excellent professor.

7. _____ I study at the university.

8. _____ The university many interesting and useful classes.

9. _____ Education is important for my family.

◇ **PRACTICE 28. Chapter review. (Chapter 6)**
Directions: Choose the correct completion for each sentence.

1. Where do _____ live?
   A. she   B. he   C. you   D. them

2. Dr. Ruiz is my dentist and neighbor. _____ is very helpful.
   A. We   B. She   C. They   D. You

3. This is our apartment. _____ is very comfortable.
   A. It   B. We   C. She   D. He

4. These are our seats. Do you want to sit next to _____?
   A. we   B. our   C. it   D. us

5. The students are going to the movies. Their teacher is taking _____.
   A. we   B. us   C. they   D. them

6. Many _____ in the neighborhood work from their homes.
   A. women   B. woman   C. womens   D. womans

7. You and _____ like to read the same books and listen to the same music.
   A. me   B. I   C. him   D. her

8. Paul is an active child. Children like to play with _____.
   A. her   B. he   C. him   D. she

9. _____ bird has a vocabulary of fifteen words.
   A. Our   B. We   C. I   D. Us

10. I love _____.
    A. China food   B. food Chinese   C. food China   D. Chinese food

CHAPTER 7
Count and Noncount Nouns

◇ **PRACTICE 1. Singular and plural. (Chart 7-1)**
Directions: Write "S" for singular or "P" for plural in front of the noun.

1. ___S___ boy   5. _____ students

2. _____ boys   6. _____ house

3. _____ car   7. _____ apartments

4. _____ teacher   8. _____ computer

◇ **PRACTICE 2. Singular and plural. (Chart 7-1)**
Directions: Write all the correct words from the list in front of each noun.

one	a	five
some	a lot of	sixty

1. ___some, a lot of, five, sixty___ telephones

2. _____ truck

3. _____ trucks

4. _____ pencil

5. _____ pencils

truck

◇ **PRACTICE 3. Count and noncount nouns. (Chart 7-1)**
Directions: Write "C" for count or "NC" for noncount in front of each noun.

1. ___C___ girls   5. _____ cars

2. _____ girl   6. _____ soup

3. _____ homework   7. _____ money

4. _____ traffic   8. _____ coin

◇ PRACTICE 4. Count and noncount nouns. (Chart 7-1)
Directions: Write all the correct words from the list in front of each noun.

some	one	ten
a	a lot of	twenty

1. ____a, one____ coin

2. _____ coins

3. _____ water

4. _____ jewelry

5. _____ cups

6. _____ ring

7. _____ rings

8. _____ advice

◇ PRACTICE 5. Count and noncount nouns. (Chart 7-1)
Directions: Complete the words with **-s** or **Ø** (nothing).

1. a book ___Ø___, one book _____, two book _____, several book _____,

   some book _____

2. a job _____, one job _____, five job _____, a lot of job _____

3. information _____, some information _____, a lot of information _____

4. a fact _____, two fact _____, several fact _____, a lot of fact _____

◇ PRACTICE 6. Count and noncount nouns. (Chart 7-1)
Directions: Circle all the words that can come before each noun.

1. a   one   (some)   (a lot of)   homework

2. a   one   some   a lot of   letter

3. a   one   some   a lot of   letters

4. a   one   some   a lot of   textbook

5. a   one   some   a lot of   table

6. a   one   some   a lot of   music

7. a   one   some   a lot of   vocabulary

8. a   one   some   a lot of   word

9. a   one   some   a lot of   words

10. a   one   some   a lot of   letters

◇ PRACTICE 7. Count and noncount nouns. (Chart 7-1)
  Directions: Write a noncount noun that is close in meaning to the count noun.

	COUNT	NONCOUNT
1.	a job	*work*
2.	an assignment (for school)	_____
3.	a song	_____
4.	a word	_____
5.	a fact	_____
6.	a suggestion	_____
7.	a chair, a desk, a table	_____
8.	a banana, an apple	_____
9.	a coin	_____
10.	a ring, a bracelet	_____

bracelet

◇ PRACTICE 8. Noun review. (Charts 6-4, 6-5, and 7-1)
  Directions: Complete each sentence with a word from the list. Make the word plural when necessary. Use each word only one time.

advice	fruit	✓money	weather
child	furniture	monkey	work
city	help	potato	
country	horse	sentence	
foot	man	traffic	

1. I have a lot of _____ *money* _____ in my wallet. I'm rich.

2. Cowboys ride _____.

3. I would like to visit many _____ in Canada. I'd like to visit

   Vancouver, Victoria, Quebec City, Toronto, and some others.

4. There are three _____ in North America: Canada, the United States,

   and Mexico.

5. I like to go to the zoo. I like to watch animals. I like to watch elephants, tigers, and

   _____.

6. There is a lot of _____ on the street during rush hour.

7. Barbara has four suitcases. She can't carry all of them. She needs

some _____ .

8. Susie and Bobby are seven years old. They aren't adults. They're

_____ .

9. We need a new bed, a new sofa, and some new chairs. We need

some new _____ .

10. People wear shoes on their _____ .

11. I like apples, oranges, and bananas. I eat a lot of _____ .

12. Sometimes I have a steak, a salad, and French-fried _____ for dinner.

13. When the temperature is around 35°C (77°F), I'm comfortable. But I don't like very hot

_____ .

14. I'm not busy today. I don't have much _____ to do.

15. I have a problem. I need your help. I need some _____ from you.

16. Some _____ have mustaches.

17. There are seventeen _____ in this exercise.

◇ PRACTICE 9. A/AN. (Chart 7-2)
   Directions: Write **a** or **an**.

1. __*an*__ idea   6. _____ interesting idea

2. _____ orange   7. _____ hour

3. _____ elephant   8. _____ house

4. _____ university 9. _____ hungry animal

5. _____ uncle   10. _____ upset child

◇ PRACTICE 10. A/AN with adjectives. (Chart 7-2)
   Directions: Write **a**, **an**, or **Ø**.

1. __*Ø*__ happy   6. _____ easy test

2. __*a*__ happy man   7. _____ honest man

3. _____ exciting   8. _____ honest

4. _____ exciting day   9. _____ my father

5. _____ hot oven   ← oven   10. _____ his job

◇ PRACTICE 11. A/AN with adjectives. (Chart 7-2)
   Directions: Write **a, an,** or **Ø**.

   1. I need to see _____*a*_____ doctor.

   2. I have _____ backache.

   3. It is _____ painful.

   4. Mary is reading _____ article in the newspaper.

   5. The article is _____ interesting.

   6. _____ healthy person gets regular exercise.

   7. The Browns own _____ house.

   8. Gary and Joel are having _____ argument in the cafeteria. It is _____ uncomfortable situation.

   9. I feel _____ uncomfortable.

   10. Are you _____ hard worker?

   11. Do you work _____ hard?

   12. Janet is _____ honest person.

   13. The store manager is talking to _____ angry woman.

   14. Bill is _____ uncle. He has _____ niece and two nephews.

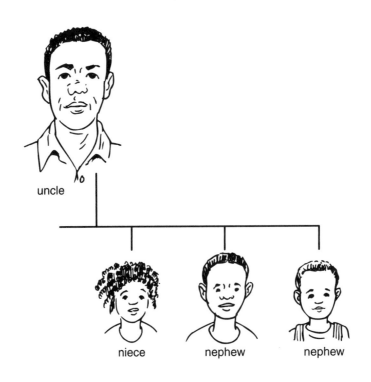

uncle

niece   nephew   nephew

◇ **PRACTICE 12. A/AN and SOME.** (Chart 7-3)
Directions: Write each word in the list in the correct column.

advice	furniture	dog	gardens	packages	elevator	umbrellas
✓ suggestion	eggs	umbrella	flower	mail	earache	letter

A	***AN***	***SOME***
_____suggestion_____	_____	_____
_____	_____	_____
_____	_____	_____
_____	[ELEVATOR]	_____
		_____
		_____
		_____

◇ **PRACTICE 13. A/AN and SOME.** (Chart 7-3)
Directions: Complete the sentences with *a/an* or *some*.

1. Here is _____a_____ letter for you.

2. There is _____ mail on the kitchen table.

3. _____ teachers give a lot of homework.

4. I have _____ long assignment.

5. The teacher has _____ interesting idea for today's discussion.

6. _____ ideas take several days to discuss.

7. Dr. Roberts is _____ very special teacher.

8. He gives _____ interesting lectures.

9. Are _____ students working on their projects?

10. Is _____ assistant teacher helping them?

◇ **PRACTICE 14. Review.** (Charts 7-1 → 7-4)
Directions: Check (✓) the incorrect sentences and correct them.

                    a
1. __✓__ I have ∧ job.

2. _____ I would like interesting job.

3. _____ Tom enjoys his works. He has a restaurant and a computer business.

4. _____ Let's listen to a music.

5. _____ Our teacher has a lot of information.

6. _____ Our teacher knows a lot of fact.

7. _____ The students want to learn more English vocabularies.

8. _____ Some English words are very difficult.

◇ PRACTICE 15. Units of measure. (Chart 7-4)
   Directions: Write the name of the item for each picture. Use the expressions in the list.

a bag of	a box of	a carton of
a bar of	a bunch of	a jar of
a bottle of	a can of	a tube of

1. ___*a bag of rice*_____

2. _____

3. _____

4. _____

5. _____

6. _____

7. _____

8. _____

9. _____

◇ PRACTICE 16. Units of measure. (Chart 7-4)
   Directions: Complete the phrases with a word from the list.

bread	cereal	ice cream	mayonnaise	rice
bananas	cheese	lettuce	✓paper	water

What can you find at a store or restaurant?

1. a sheet of _____ *paper* _____

2. a head of _____

3. a box of _____

4. a piece of _____

5. a loaf of _____

6. a bunch of _____

7. a bowl of _____

8. a bottle of _____

9. a jar of _____

◇ PRACTICE 17. Review: A/AN/SOME and units of measure. (Charts 7-3 and 7-4)
   Directions: Complete the sentences with *a*, *an*, or *some*.

1. I'm hungry. I'd like . . .

   a. _____ *a* _____ piece of chicken.

   b. _____ fruit

   c. _____ food

   d. _____ bananas

   e. _____ orange

   f. _____ sandwich

   g. _____ rice

   h. _____ ice cream

2. I'm thirsty. I'd like . . .

   a. _____ *some* _____ water

   b. _____ bottle of water

   c. _____ juice

d. _____ glass of milk

e. _____ cup of coffee

f. _____ strong coffee

g. _____ tea

h. _____ milk

◇ PRACTICE 18. MUCH/MANY. (Chart 7-5)
Directions: Complete the sentences with **much** or **many**.

I need to go to the store. I don't have . . .

1. ____*much*____ coffee   6. _____ sugar

2. _____ bananas   7. _____ bread

3. _____ fruit   8. _____ food

4. _____ lamb   9. _____ apples

5. _____ rice   10. _____ cans of soup

◇ PRACTICE 19. A FEW/A LITTLE. (Chart 7-5)
Directions: Complete the sentences with **a few** or **a little**.

I need to go shopping. I need . . .

1. ____*a little*____ salt   7. _____ bottles of water

2. _____ oranges   8. _____ sandwiches

3. _____ pens   9. _____ flour

4. _____ cheese   10. _____ rolls of toilet paper

5. _____ tea

6. _____ teabags   teabag

◇ PRACTICE 20. MUCH/MANY/A FEW/A LITTLE. (Chart 7-5)
Directions: Circle the correct words. Add **-s** or **Ø** (nothing) to the nouns where necessary.

1. The teacher needs *a few,* (*a little*) information ___Ø___ about her students.

2. Do the students have *much,* (*many*) question ___s___?

3. Here are a *few, a little* new pen _____ for you.

4. Do you have *a few, a little* minute _____ to talk?

5. Andy doesn't drink *much, many* coffee _____. He drinks *a few, a little* _____ tea.

6. There are *much, many* beautiful flowers _____ in your garden.

7. I have *a few, a little* flower _____ in my garden and *much, many* vegetable _____.

◇ PRACTICE 21. HOW MUCH/HOW MANY. (Chart 7-5)
   Directions: Rick is going shopping. His wife gives him a list. He needs to know the amount to buy. Write questions with *How much/How many . . . do we need?*

cheese	*eggs*	*carrots*
olive oil	*fruit*	*flour*

1. ____How much cheese do we need?_____

2. _____

3. _____

4. _____

5. _____

6. _____

◇ PRACTICE 22. Using THE. (Chart 7-6)
   Directions: Complete the sentences with *the* where necessary.

1. Elizabeth is standing outside. It's midnight.

   a. She's looking up at ___the___ sky.

   b. She sees _____ moon.

   c. She doesn't see _____ sun.

   d. _____ stars are very bright.

   e. _____ planets are difficult to find.

2. Sarah is on the phone, describing her new kitchen to a friend.

   a. ___The___ phone is on the wall above ___the___ counter.

   b. _____ dishwasher is next to _____ sink.

   c. _____ stove and refrigerator are near each other.

   d. _____ window is above _____ sink.

   e. _____ wallpaper has blue and yellow stripes.

3. Scott is on the phone, describing his living room to a friend.

a. __*The*__ TV is across from _____ sofa.

b. _____ coffee table is in front of _____ sofa.

c. _____ stereo is against _____ wall.

d. _____ bookshelves are near _____ TV.

◇ PRACTICE 23. First mention vs. second mention. (Chart 7-6)
Directions: Complete the sentences with **the** or **a**.

1. These pants and shirts don't fit. __*The*__ pants are too big, and _____ shirts are too tight.

2. Here's some chicken. Watch out! _____ chicken is very spicy.

3. Andrew drives _____ company truck. _____ truck is big, and uses a lot of gas. His company pays for _____ gas.

4. Rudy wants to give his wife _____ ring for their anniversary. _____ ring has three diamonds, and _____ diamonds are very large.

5. Rachel is looking at _____ picture of _____ dog and _____ baby. _____ baby is sleeping, and _____ dog is watching her.

6. Tommy is getting _____ new bike for his birthday. _____ bike is very fast, and he is excited to ride it.

◇ PRACTICE 24. General vs. specific. (Chart 7-7)
Directions: Decide if the word in *italics* has a general or specific meaning.

1. *Clothes* are expensive.	(general)	specific
2. The *clothes* in Jan's closet are expensive.	general	specific
3. *Lemons* are sour.	general	specific
4. I love *vegetables.*	general	specific
5. The *vegetables* on the counter are from my garden.	general	specific
6. How are the *carrots* in your salad? Are they sweet?	general	specific
7. *Rabbits* like carrots.	general	specific
8. What are you doing about the *rabbits* in your garden?	general	specific

◇ **PRACTICE 25. Using THE. (Chart 7-7)**
Directions: Complete the sentences with *a/an*, *the*, or **Ø** (nothing).

1. I need _____Ø_____ sugar for my coffee.

2. _____ sugar is in the cupboard.

3. Dentists say _____ sugar is not good for our teeth.

4. I'd like _____ glass of water.

5. Ann would like _____ orange for a snack.

6. _____ oranges grow on trees.

7. Ken has _____ egg every day for lunch.

8. Are _____ eggs healthy?

9. I'm going shopping. I need _____ bread and _____ cheese.

10. Jack is having _____ rice, _____ fish, and _____ bowl of soup for dinner.

11. _____ cat from next door is sitting on your front porch. He smells _____ fish
    you are cooking.

12. Do you like _____ cats? Would you like _____ cat?

◇ **PRACTICE 26. Article review. (Charts 7-3, 7-6, and 7-7)**
Directions: Choose the sentence that is closest in meaning to the given situation.

1. Mark is at a toy store. There are five fire trucks. He buys one.
   (A.) He buys a fire truck.   B. He buys the fire truck.

2. Pat is at a toy store. There is only one doll left. She
   buys it.
       A. She buys a doll.   B. She buys the doll.

3. Victor is at a DVD rental store. There are thousands of movies
   to rent. He chooses four.
       A. He rents the DVDs.   B. He rents some DVDs.

4. Martha is at the library. There is one book about Nelson Mandela.
       A. She checks out the book about Nelson Mandela.
       B. She checks out a book about Nelson Mandela.

5. Jane is sitting outside in her garden. It is midnight. She is looking up at the sky.
       A. She sees the moon.
       B. She sees a moon.

6. I love animals. Horses are my favorite.
    A. I love the horses.   B. I love horses.

7. There are fifty cars in a parking lot. Ten cars are white.
    A. The cars in the parking lot are white.
    B. Some cars in the parking lot are white.

8. Alice is picking apples from an apple tree. It has only five apples. She picks all five.
    A. She takes the apples home.   B. She takes some apples home.

9. Paul drives a small car. He wants to save gas.
    A. He doesn't like to drive big cars.   B. He doesn't like to drive the big cars.

◇ PRACTICE 27. SOME/ANY. (Chart 7-8)
    Directions: Circle the correct word. In some cases, both words are correct.

    1. Let's go outside. I need (some,) any fresh air.

    2. There aren't *some, any* clouds in the sky.

    3. There is *some, any* wind.

    4. I don't feel *some, any* wind.

    5. Do you have *some, any* time?

    6. Sorry, I don't have *some, any*   time right now.

    7. I have *some, any*   time tomorrow.

    8. I need *some, any*   money for the store.

    9. Do you have *some, any*   money?

    10. *Some, Any*   people carry a lot of money in their wallets.

◇ PRACTICE 28. SOME/ANY. (Charts 7-3 and 7-8)
    Directions: Think about shopping. Write sentences about what you need and don't need.
    Use ***some/any*** and the words from the list. Add ***-s/-es*** where necessary. You can also use
    your own words.

egg	*flour*	*banana*	*soap*	*fruit*
rice	*potato*	*coffee*	*orange*	*vegetable*
fish	*apple*	*toothpaste*	*soup*	*meat*

    1. I need _____, _____,

       _____, _____, and

       _____.

2. I don't need _____, _____,

_____, _____, or

_____.

◇ **PRACTICE 29. Chapter review.** (Chart 7-1 → 7-8)
Directions: Correct the errors.

    countries
1. Korea and Japan are ~~country~~ in Asia.

2. Is there many traffics at 5:00 P.M.?

3. Are you a hungry? Could I get you some food?

4. My children come home with a lot of homeworks.

5. The digital cameras take wonderful pictures.

6. My eggs and coffee don't taste very good. Eggs are very salty, and coffee is weak.

7. What do you like better for a snack: orange or the orange juice?

8. I buy the jeans every year.

9. I'm going to bank. I need money.

10. We need to get any furniture. Do you know good furniture store?

CHAPTER 8

Expressing Past Time, Part 1

◇ PRACTICE 1. Past forms of BE. (Chart 8-1)

Directions: Complete the sentences with the correct form of *be*.

Now . . .

An hour ago . . .

1. I am tired.   I _____*was*_____ tired.

2. we are tired.   we _____ tired.

3. she is tired.   she _____ tired.

4. they are tired. they _____ tired.

5. he is tired.   he _____ tired.

6. the cat is tired. the cat _____ tired.

7. my children are tired. my children _____ tired.

8. Al and Todd are tired. Al and Todd _____ tired.

9. our teacher is tired. our teacher _____ tired.

10. you are tired. you _____ tired.

◇ PRACTICE 2. Past forms of BE. (Chart 8-1)

Directions: Choose the correct form of the verb in each sentence.

1. My parents   *was,* (*were*) at home last night.

2. Our next-door neighbors   *was, were*   at a concert.

3. I   *was, were*   at the library.

4. My roommate   *was, were*   there too.

5. She   *was, were*   across the table from me.

6. Our teacher   *was, were*   at the table next to us.

7. He   *was, were*   asleep.

8. We   *was, were*   at the library until closing time.

9. The library   *was, were*   open until 9:00 P.M.

◇ **PRACTICE 3. Past forms of BE: negative. (Chart 8-2)**
　　Directions: Complete the sentences with the correct negative form: ***wasn't*** or ***weren't***.

　　1. I _____ *wasn't* _____ at school yesterday.

　　2. You _____ at school yesterday.

　　3. Some students _____ at school yesterday.

　　4. They _____ at school yesterday.

　　5. Toshi _____ at school yesterday.

　　6. He _____ at school yesterday.

　　7. My teacher _____ at school yesterday.

　　8. Beth and Mark _____ at school yesterday.

　　9. Sarah _____ at school yesterday.

　10. She and I _____ at school yesterday.

　11. We _____ at school yesterday.

◇ **PRACTICE 4. Past tense of BE: negative. (Chart 8-2)**
　　Directions: Complete the sentences with the correct negative form: ***wasn't*** or ***weren't***.

　　1. The hotel _____ *wasn't* _____ expensive.

　　2. The concert tickets _____ cheap.

　　3. I _____ happy about that.

　　4. My parents _____ in town last week.

　　5. My teacher _____ at school yesterday afternoon.

　　6. Many students _____ in class last week.

　　7. They _____ well.

　　8. The bird _____ in her cage this morning.

　　9. The cage door _____ closed.

◇ **PRACTICE 5. Past tense of BE: negative. (Chart 8-2)**
  Directions: Write sentences about the people in the chart.

	MIKE	LORI	RICARDO	EVA
at work	x			
at school				
on vacation			x	
out of town		x		x

Where were they yesterday?

1. Mike _____ *wasn't out of town yesterday. He was at work.* _____

2. Ricardo _____

3. Lori _____

4. Lori and Eva _____

◇ **PRACTICE 6. Past tense of BE: negative. (Chart 8-2)**
  Directions: Think about your elementary school years. Write sentences about yourself. Use
  was or ***wasn't***.

1. *(shy)* _____ *I was / wasn't shy.* _____

2. *(happy)* _____

3. *(quiet)* _____

4. *(active)* _____

5. *(serious)* _____

6. *(noisy)* _____

◇ **PRACTICE 7. Past tense of BE: questions. (Chart 8-3)**
  Directions: Complete the questions with ***Was*** or ***Were***.

1. _____ *Were* _____ you home yesterday evening?

2. _____ your husband home yesterday evening?

3. _____ he home yesterday evening?

4. _____ your parents home last weekend?

5. _____ they home last weekend?

6. _____ I home last weekend?

7. _____ the teacher home last night?

8. _____ your teacher home last night?

9. _____ Jan and I home yesterday evening?

10. _____ we home last weekend?

◇ **PRACTICE 8. Past tense of BE: questions.** (Chart 8-3)

Directions: Make two questions for each situation. The first question is yes/no, and the second is a ***where*** question. Give the answers for both questions. Use the places in the list.

at the zoo	*at the mall*	*at the train station*
at the library	*at home*	*at the grocery store*

1. Jake and Kevin \ at a movie theater

   A: _____*Were Jake and Kevin at a movie theater?*_____

   B: _____*No, they weren't.*_____

   A: _____*Where were they?*_____

   B: _____*They were at the grocery store.*_____

2. Ellen \ at the library

   A: _____

   B: _____

   A: _____

   B: _____

3. you \ at a party

   A: _____

   B: _____

   A: _____

   B: _____

4. Thomas \ at the airport

   A: _____

   B: _____

   A: _____

   B: _____

5. your children \ at school

A: _____

B: _____

A: _____

B: _____

6. Liz and you \ at the park

A: _____

B: _____

A: _____

B: _____

◇ PRACTICE 9. Past tense of BE: questions. (Chart 8-3)

Directions: Your friend was at a movie last night. Ask questions about the movie. Use ***was*** or ***were***.

1. _____*Was*_____ it scary?

2. _____ you afraid?

3. _____ the characters interesting?

4. _____ the movie funny?

5. _____ the main actor good?

6. _____ she or he a good actor?

7. _____ the actors good?

8. _____ they good?

◇ PRACTICE 10. Past tense -ED. (Chart 8-4)

Directions: Complete the sentences with the past tense form of the verbs.

Every day . . .

1. I study English.

2. he studies English.

3. we walk in the park.

4. you work hard.

5. they smile.

6. the baby smiles.

Yesterday . . .

I _____*studied*_____ English.

he _____ English.

we _____ in the park.

you _____ hard.

they _____ .

the baby _____ .

Every day . . .	Yesterday . . .
7. Sonja talks on the phone.	Sonja _____ on the phone.
8. Tim helps his parents.	Tim _____ his parents.
9. I help my parents.	I _____ my parents.
10. she listens carefully.	she _____ carefully.
11. they listen carefully.	they _____ carefully.

◇ **PRACTICE 11. Past tense -ED. (Chart 8-4)**
   Directions: Look at the activities and write sentences about the people.

YESTERDAY	RUTH	DEB	BILL	STUART
cook breakfast	x		x	
watch TV		x	x	
talk to friends on the phone	x			
exercise at a gym				x

1. Deb ___*watched TV.*_____

2. Stuart _____

3. Ruth and Bill _____

4. Ruth also _____

5. Bill also _____

◇ PRACTICE 12. Pronunciation practice: -ED verbs. (Chart 8-4)
Directions: Read the words aloud. Then use the words to complete the sentences.

GROUP A: Final *-ed* is pronounced /t/ after voiceless sounds. Practice saying these words.

walked	asked	washed	erased	laughed
worked	✓watched	finished	helped	coughed
cooked	touched	kissed	stopped	

1. I _____watched_____ TV last night.

2. Anna _____ to class yesterday instead of taking the bus.

3. I _____ the dirty dishes after dinner last night.

4. Jim _____ the board with an eraser.

5. Robert loves his daughter. He _____ her on the forehead.

6. The joke was funny. We _____ at the funny story.

7. The rain _____ a few minutes ago. The sky is clear now.

8. I worked for three hours last night. I _____ my homework about nine o'clock.

9. Steve _____ my shoulder with his hand to get my attention.

10. Mr. Wilson _____ in his garden yesterday morning.

11. Judy _____ a lot. She had a bad cold.

12. Dan is a good cook. He _____ some delicious food last night.

13. Linda _____ a question in class yesterday.

14. I had a problem with my homework. The teacher _____ me before class.

GROUP B: Final *-ed* is pronounced /d/ after voiced sounds. Practice saying these words.

rained	arrived	sneezed	played
signed	smiled	closed	enjoyed
shaved	killed	remembered	snowed

15. It's winter. The ground is white because it _____snowed_____ yesterday.

16. Anita _____ at the airport on September 3.

17. The girls and boys _____ baseball after school yesterday.

18. When Ali got a new credit card, he _____ his name in ink on the back of the card.

19. Rick used to have a beard, but now he doesn't. He _____ it this morning.

20. The students' test papers were very good. The teacher, Mr. Jackson, was very pleased.

    He _____ when he returned the test papers.

21. I _____ the party last night. It was fun. I had a good time.

22. The window was open. Mr. Chan _____ it because it was cold outside.

23. The streets were wet this morning because it _____ last night.

24. "Achoo!" When Judy _____, Ken said, "Bless you." Oscar said, "Gesundheit!"

25. I have my books with me. I didn't forget them today. I _____ to bring them to class.

26. Mrs. Lane was going crazy because there was a fly in the room. The fly was buzzing all around the room. Finally, she _____ it with a rolled-up newspaper.

GROUP C: Final **-ed** is pronounced /əd/ after /t/ and /d/. Practice saying these words.

waited	counted	invited	added
✓ wanted	visited	needed	folded

27. The children ____wanted____ some candy after dinner.

28. Mr. Miller _____ to stay in the hospital for two weeks after he had an operation.

29. I _____ the number of students in the room. There were twenty.

30. Mr. and Mrs. Johnson _____ us to come to their house last Sunday.

31. Last Sunday we _____ the Johnsons. We had dinner with them.

32. I _____ the letter before I put it in the envelope.

33. Kim _____ for the bus at the corner of

    Fifth Avenue and Main Street.

34. The boy _____ the numbers on the board

    in math class yesterday.

CHART 8-A: SUMMARY OF SPELLING RULES FOR -ED VERBS

	END OF VERB →	-ED FORM
Rule 1:	END OF VERB: A CONSONANT + -e → smile erase	ADD -d. smiled erased
Rule 2:	ONE VOWEL + ONE CONSONANT → stop rub	DOUBLE THE CONSONANT. ADD -ed. stopped rubbed
Rule 3:	TWO VOWELS + ONE CONSONANT → rain need	ADD -ed. DO NOT DOUBLE THE CONSONANT. rained needed
Rule 4:	TWO CONSONANTS → count help	ADD -ed. DO NOT DOUBLE THE CONSONANT. counted helped
Rule 5:	CONSONANT + -y → study carry	CHANGE -y TO -i. ADD -ed. studied carried
Rule 6:	VOWEL + -y → play enjoy	ADD -ed. DO NOT CHANGE -y TO -i. played enjoyed

*EXCEPTIONS: Do not double **x** (*fix* + *-ed* = *fixed*). Do not double **w** (*snow* + *-ed* = *snowed*).

◇ PRACTICE 13. Spelling rules: -ED verbs. (Chart 8-A)
    Directions: Study each rule and the examples. Then write the past tense of the given verbs.

    Rule 1. END OF VERB: A CONSONANT + -e → ADD -d.

      1. like   → _____

      2. close   → _____

      3. shave   → _____

      4. love   → _____

      5. hate   → _____

      6. exercise → _____

Rule 2. ONE VOWEL + ONE CONSONANT → DOUBLE THE CONSONANT. ADD *-ed*.

7. plan   →   _____

8. drop   →   _____

9. clap   →   _____

Rule 3. TWO VOWELS + ONE CONSONANT → ADD *-ed*. DO NOT DOUBLE THE CONSONANT.

10. join   →   _____

11. shout   →   _____

12. wait   →   _____

Rule 4. TWO CONSONANTS → ADD *-ed*. DO NOT DOUBLE THE CONSONANT.

13. point   →   _____

14. touch   →   _____

15. melt   →   _____

Rule 5. CONSONANT + *-y* → CHANGE *-y* TO *-i*. ADD *-ed*.

16. marry   →   _____

17. try   →   _____

18. hurry   →   _____

19. reply   →   _____

20. dry   →   _____

Rule 6. VOWEL + *-y* → ADD *-ed*. DO NOT CHANGE *-y* TO *-i*.

21. stay   →   _____

22. delay   →   _____

NOTE: Spelling rules for the 2-syllable verbs *visit, answer, happen, occur, listen, open,* and *enter* are in Appendix 6 at the back of this text.

◇ **PRACTICE 14. Spelling practice: -ED. (Chart 8-4)**
   Directions: Write the **-ed** forms of these verbs.

	-ED
1. count	_____counted_____
2. rain	_____
3. help	_____
4. plan	_____
5. dream	_____
6. erase	_____
7. close	_____
8. yawn	_____
9. study	_____
10. worry	_____
11. drop	_____

◇ **PRACTICE 15. Spelling review: -ED. (Chart 8-4)**
   Directions: Use the correct form of the words in the list to complete the sentences.

carry	enjoy	learn	stay	wait
clap	fail	rub	stop	
cry	✓finish	smile	taste	

1. I ____finished____ my homework at nine o'clock last night.

2. We _____ some new vocabulary yesterday.

3. I _____ the soup before dinner last night. It was delicious.

4. Linda _____ for the bus at the corner yesterday.

5. The bus _____ at the corner. It was on time.

6. We _____ the play at the theater last night. It was very good.

7. At the theater last night, the audience _____
   when the play was over.

8. Ann _____ her suitcases to the bus
   station yesterday. They weren't heavy.

9. The baby _____ her eyes because she was sleepy.

10. I _____ home and watched a sad movie on TV last night. I

_____ at the end of the movie.

11. Mike _____ his examination last week. His grade was 0%.

12. Jane _____ at the children. She was happy to see them.

◇ **PRACTICE 16. YESTERDAY, LAST, AGO. (Chart 8-5)**
Directions: Complete the sentences with **yesterday**, **last**, or **ago**.

The children played soccer . . .

1. ____*last*____ night.

2. _____ afternoon.

3. _____ Wednesday.

4. _____ week.

5. _____ summer.

6. _____ month.

7. _____ evening.

8. three months _____.

9. two weeks _____.

10. one year _____.

11. _____ morning.

12. _____ weekend.

◇ **PRACTICE 17. YESTERDAY, LAST, AGO. (Chart 8-5)**
Directions: Rewrite each *italicized* sentence using time expressions with **yesterday**, **last**, or **ago**.

1. It's 7:00. *At 6:55, Tim brushed his teeth.*

____*Tim brushed his teeth five minutes ago.*____

2. It's 3:00 P.M. *The day before at 3:00, Bonnie walked to the park.*

_____

3. This week Tom is working. *The week before, he was at home on vacation.*

_____

4. It's 2006. *In 2002, Sam graduated from high school.*

_____

5. It's Saturday. *The Thursday before, Jan worked 12 hours.*

_____

6. It's March. *The month before, Thomas stayed with his parents.*

_____

7. It's 10:00 P.M. *The night before at 10:00, we watched a DVD.*

_____

◇ **PRACTICE 18. Irregular verbs: Group 1. (Chart 8-6)**

Directions: Complete the sentences with the past tense form of the verb.

Every day . . .   Yesterday . . .

1. I eat vegetables.   I ____*ate*____ vegetables.

2. you eat vegetables.   you _____ vegetables.

3. he eats vegetables.   he _____ vegetables.

4. she eats vegetables.   she _____ vegetables.

5. we eat vegetables.   we _____ vegetables.

6. they eat vegetables.   they _____ vegetables.

7. Sam and I eat vegetables.   Sam and I _____ vegetables.

8. I do homework.   I _____ my homework.

9. you do homework.   you _____ your homework.

10. she does homework.   she _____ her homework.

11. we do homework.   we _____ our homework.

12. I sleep eight hours.   I _____ eight hours.

13. they sleep eight hours.   they _____ eight hours.

14. we sleep eight hours.   we _____ eight hours.

15. she sleeps eight hours.   she _____ eight hours.

◇ **PRACTICE 19. Irregular verbs: Group 1. (Chart 8-6)**

Directions: Check (✓) the sentences that are true for you. Write the present form for each verb.

PRESENT FORM

1. _____ I *got* a package in the mail yesterday.   ____*get*____

2. _____ I *came* home early yesterday.   _____

3. _____ I *went* out to dinner last night.   _____

4. _____ I *had* a headache yesterday.   _____

5. _____ I *put* on sunglasses yesterday.   _____

6. _____ I *slept* for nine hours last night.   _____

7. _____ I *saw* my parents yesterday.   _____

8. _____ I *did* homework last night.   _____

9. _____ I *ate* fish for dinner.   _____

10. _____ I *wrote* an e-mail last night.   _____

11. _____ I *sat* in the sun yesterday.   _____

12. _____ I *stood* outside in the rain yesterday.   _____

◇ **PRACTICE 20. Irregular verbs: Group 1. (Chart 8-6)**

Directions: Complete the sentences with the past tense form of a verb. In some sentences, more than one verb fits. The number in parentheses tells you how many verbs you can use.

come	*eat*	*go*	*put*	*sit*	*stand*
✓*do*	*get*	*have*	*see*	*sleep*	*write*

1. Last week, I _____*did*_____ something really fun. (1)

2. I _____ to the mountains for a camping trip. (1)

3. First, I _____ outside under the stars at night. (3)

4. I _____ millions of stars in the sky. (1)

5. I also _____ three fish from the river with my fishing pole. (1)

6. I cooked them over a fire, and _____ them for dinner. (2)

7. One day I walked in the woods for several hours.

   I _____ deer and foxes with my binoculars. (1)

8. I _____ home late Monday night. (3)

9. I _____ a postcard to my parents. (1)

10. I _____ the postcard in the mail. (1)

◇ **PRACTICE 21. Simple past: negative. (Charts 1-5 and 8-7)**
Directions: Complete each sentence with the negative form of the verb.

1. I came home late.   I _____*didn't come*_____ home late.

2. You came home late.   You _____ home late.

3. He came home late.   He _____ home late.

4. She came home late.   She _____ home late.

5. We came home late.   We _____ home late.

6. They came home late.   They _____ home late.

7. He played soccer.   He _____ soccer.

8. They played soccer.   They _____ soccer.

9. She answered the phone.   She _____ the phone.

10. I saw a movie.   I _____ a movie.

11. You slept late.   You _____ late.

12. I did my homework.   I _____ my homework.

13. I was late.   I _____ late.

14. They were late.   They _____ late.

◇ **PRACTICE 22. Simple past: negative. (Chart 8-7)**
Directions: Write sentences that are true for you.

1. eat \ a big dinner \ last night

    _____*I ate a big dinner last night.*_ OR _*I didn't eat a big dinner last night.*_____

2. sleep \ on the floor \ last night

    _____

3. write \ an e-mail \ last week

    _____

4. walk \ to school \ last month

    _____

5. get \ some money from the bank \ yesterday

    _____

6. go \ to my cousins' \ last week

    _____

7. do \ some housework (cleaning) \ yesterday

_____

8. work \ in the garden \ yesterday

_____

9. put on \ my shoes \ yesterday

_____

◇ PRACTICE 23. Simple past: negative (Chart 8-7)
Directions: Read the story about Jack. Look at the sentences. If the sentence is true, do not change it. If it is wrong, write the negative.

   Yesterday, my alarm clock didn't go off. I jumped out of bed, and looked at the clock. It was 7:45! I was late for work. I hurried to the kitchen and quickly prepared breakfast. I had some juice and toast. After breakfast, I put the dishes in the sink. I didn't have time to wash them. Then I quickly got dressed. Twenty minutes later, I was ready. I walked to the bus. At the bus stop, I didn't recognize anyone. Then I looked at my watch. It was 6:30. I thought it was 8:30. I was two hours early!

1. His alarm clock went off. _____*His alarm clock didn't go off.*_____

2. He got out of bed quickly. _____*(no change)*_____

3. He cooked a big breakfast. _____

4. He washed the dishes. _____

5. He got dressed in a hurry. _____

6. He saw his friends at the bus stop. _____

7. He was late for work. _____

8. It was time for work. _____

◇ **PRACTICE 24. Simple past: Yes/no questions. (Chart 8-8)**

Directions: Read the story. Then write the questions the doctor asked John, and give John's answers.

John didn't feel well. He went to see Dr. Jones. Dr. Jones checked him, and asked him about his lifestyle. John had several unhealthy habits: he worked every day, he didn't exercise, he ate unhealthy foods, and he smoked. He needed to change these habits. John listened to the doctor, but he didn't change any habits. He went back to the doctor after a few months. The doctor asked him several questions.

1. Dr. Jones: *you \ quit smoking?*
   <u>   Did you quit smoking?   </u>   John: <u>   No, I didn't.   </u>

2. Dr. Jones: *you \ eat \ more healthy foods?*
   _____   John: _____

3. Dr. Jones: *you \ exercise \ three times a week?*
   _____   John: _____

4. Dr. Jones: *you \ take \ more vacation time?*
   _____   John: _____

5. Dr. Jones: *you \ work \ seven days a week?*
   _____   John: _____

◇ **PRACTICE 25. Review of yes/no questions: past and present. (Charts 3-10 and 8-8)**

Directions: Make yes/no questions.

1. <u>   Do they play   </u>   tennis?   Yes, they do. They play tennis.

2. _____   tennis?   Yes, they did. They played tennis.

3. _____   tennis?   Yes, she does. She plays tennis.

4. _____   tennis?   Yes, she did. She played tennis.

5. _____   to work?   Yes, he does. He walks to work.

6. _____   to work?   Yes, he did. He walked to work.

7. _____   at home?   Yes, she does. She works at home.

8. _____   at home?   Yes, she did. She worked at home.

9. _____   your new job? Yes, I do. I like my new job.

10. _____   your old job? Yes, I did. I liked my old job.

◇ PRACTICE 26. Yes/no questions. (Charts 8-3 and 8-8)
Directions: Complete the sentences with *did, was,* or *were.*

Tell me about your trip.

1. _____*Did*_____ you have a good time?

2. _____ it fun?

3. _____ you see a lot of interesting sights?

4. _____ you meet many people?

5. _____ the people friendly?

6. _____ you learn a lot?

7. _____ the trip long enough?

8. _____ you want to come home?

9. _____ you ready to come home?

◇ PRACTICE 27. Review: questions and negatives. (Charts 8-7 and 8-8)
Directions: Make questions and negative sentences from the given words.

		QUESTION	NEGATIVE
1. a.	They play.	*Do they play?*	*They don't play.*
b.	They played.	*Did they play?*	*They didn't play?*
2. a.	They help.	_____	_____
b.	They helped.	_____	_____
3. a.	She listens.	_____	_____
b.	She listened.	_____	_____
4. a.	He works.	_____	_____
b.	He worked.	_____	_____
5. a.	The baby cries.	_____	_____
b.	The baby cried.	_____	_____
6. a.	We are sick.	_____	_____
b.	We were sick.	_____	_____

◇ PRACTICE 28. Review: Yes/no questions. (Charts 8-2, 8-3, 8-7, and 8-8)
Directions: Make yes/no questions. Give short answers.

1. A: _____*Were you at home last night?*_____

    B: _____*No, I wasn't*_____ (I wasn't at home last night.)

    A: _____*Did you go to a movie?*_____

    B: _____*Yes, I did.*_____ (I went to a movie.)

2. A: _____

    B: _____ (It isn't cold today.)

3. A: _____

    B: _____ (I come to class every day.)

4. A: _____

    B: _____ (Roberto was absent yesterday.)

5. A: _____

    B: _____ (Roberto stayed home yesterday.)

6. A: _____

    B: _____ (My family doesn't watch television every day.)

7. A: _____

    B: _____ (Mohammed isn't in class today.)

8. A: _____

    B: _____ (He was here yesterday.)

9. A: _____

    B: _____ (He came to class the day before yesterday.)

10. A: _____

    B: _____ (He usually comes to class every day.)

◇ PRACTICE 29. Irregular verbs: Group 2. (Chart 8-9)
Directions: Check (✓) the sentences that are true for you. Write the present form for each verb.

PRESENT FORM

1. _____ I *bought* some snack food yesterday.   _____*buy*_____

2. _____ I *read* a newspaper last week.   _____

3. _____ I *rode* a horse last year.   _____

4. _____ I *ran* up some stairs yesterday.   _____

5. _____ I *drank* tea yesterday. _____

6. _____ I *caught* a taxi last week. _____

7. _____ I *drove* a car yesterday. _____

8. _____ I *thought* about English yesterday evening. _____

9. _____ I *brought* this book to school last week. _____

10. _____ My English books *taught* me new vocabulary last week. _____

◇ PRACTICE 30. Irregular verbs: Group 2. (Chart 8-9)
Directions: Complete each sentence with the past tense form of a verb from the list. The number in parentheses tells you how many verbs you can use.

read	ride	drink	catch	buy
think	run	teach	bring	drive

Jane is a teacher.

1. She didn't drive to work yesterday. She _____*rode*_____ her bike to school. (1)

2. In the morning, she _____ math and science to her students. (1)

3. At lunch time, she went home and got her car. She _____ her car to the mall. (1)

4. She _____ a sweater for her husband at a clothes store. (1)

5. She stopped at a cafe and _____ some coffee. (2)

6. Then she went home and _____ her students' science projects. (1)

7. Before dinner, she put on her running clothes and shoes. She walked outside and _____ down the street to the store. (1)

8. During her run, she _____ about her favorite foods: potato chips, ice cream, and chocolate. (1)

9. But she _____ home healthy foods: chicken, rice, and vegetables. (1)

10. Her husband _____ a cold last week, and she wants to stay healthy. (1)

◇ PRACTICE 31. Irregular verbs: Group 3. (Chart 8-10)
Directions: Check (✓) the sentences that are true for you. Write the present form for each verb.

1. _____ I *flew* in a small airplane last year. _____*fly*_____

2. _____ I *spoke* a little English two years ago. _____

3. _____ I *took* the bus to school last week.   _____

4. _____ I *paid* bills last month.   _____

5. _____ I *woke up* early this morning.   _____

6. _____ I *broke* my arm when I was a child.   _____

7. _____ I *sent* an e-mail to a friend last week.   _____

8. _____ I *sang* a song this morning.   _____

9. _____ I *left* my home today.   _____

10. _____ I *met* a famous person once.   _____

11. _____ A cell phone *rang* in my English class last week.   _____

12. _____ I *heard* a funny story yesterday.   _____

◇ **PRACTICE 32. Irregular verbs: Group 3. (Chart 8-10)**

Directions: Complete each sentence with the past tense form of a verb from the list. There is only one correct verb for each sentence.

hear	*leave*	*pay*	*sing*	*speak*	*meet*
take	✓*fly*	*break*	*wake up*	*send*	*ring*

1. It was 7:00 A.M. Jerry was asleep. A bird _____*flew*_____ into his open bedroom window.

2. Jerry _____ a noise.

3. The noise _____ him up. He saw the bird.

4. The bird looked hurt. Jerry _____ the bird to the veterinarian.★

5. A nurse _____ Jerry in the parking lot and helped Jerry with the bird.

6. Jerry _____ the bird at the vet's office and went to work.

7. An hour later, Jerry's office phone _____. It was the vet.

8. The vet _____ to Jerry. He said, "The bird _____ its wing, but it's okay."

9. Jerry took the bird home. After its wing was better, Jerry put it outside. The bird _____ a few songs and flew away. Jerry watched his little friend, feeling both happy and sad.

_____
★*veterinarian (vet)* = an animal doctor.

10. The vet _____ Jerry a bill for a small amount.

11. Jerry happily _____ the bill.

◇ **PRACTICE 33. Irregular verbs: Group 4. (Chart 8-11)**
Directions: Check (✓) the sentences that are true for you. Write the present form for each verb in *italics*.

		PRESENT FORM
1. _____	I *wore* a hat yesterday.	*wear*
2. _____	I *said* "Good morning" to my teacher yesterday.	_____
3. _____	I *found* money on the street last week.	_____
4. _____	I *lost* something expensive in the past.	_____
5. _____	Someone *stole* something expensive from me once.	_____
6. _____	I *hung* up my clothes before I went to bed last night.	_____
7. _____	I *told* a funny joke last week.	_____
8. _____	My classes *began* on time last week.	_____
9. _____	I *sold* something on the Internet.	_____
10. _____	The last time I paid bills, I *tore* up a check.	_____

◇ **PRACTICE 34. Irregular verbs: Group 4. (Chart 8-11)**
Directions: Complete each sentence with the past tense form of a verb from the list. There is only one correct verb for each sentence. Note the use of **tell** and **say**: **tell** + person but **say** + **to** + person.

tell	tear	✓begin	hang	sell
steal	say	find	lose	wear

1. Martha's school day _____*began*_____ with bad news.

2. Her husband said, "The dog _____ your students' work into small pieces. Now he's looking at your leather jacket."

3. Martha _____ her leather jacket to school every day. It was her favorite jacket.

4. She picked up her jacket and the homework, and _____ the dog, "No."

5. She went to school. She took off her jacket and _____ it up on a hanger in the closet.

6. At the end of the day, there was no jacket. A student _____ to her, "Maybe a thief _____ it."

7. Someone else said, "Maybe you left it somewhere else and don't remember. Maybe you _____ it."

8. Martha wondered, "Did someone steal it? Maybe someone _____ it for money."

9. An hour later, another student _____ Martha's jacket in the closet. It was on a hanger under another teacher's jacket!

◇ PRACTICE 35. Review: -ED spelling.
Directions: Write the correct spelling of the **-ed** form.

	-ED FORM			**-ED** FORM
1. wait	*waited*	9. point	
2. spell	*spelled*	10. pat	
3. kiss	*kissed*	11. shout	
4. plan	_____	12. reply	
5. join	_____	13. play	
6. hope	_____	14. touch	
7. drop	_____	15. end	
8. add	_____	16. dance	

◇ PRACTICE 36. Review: -ED pronunciation.
Directions: Circle the correct pronunciation of the **-ed** form: /t/, /d/, or /əd/.

1. walked	(/t/)	/d/	/əd/
2. stayed	/t/	/d/	/əd/
3. stopped	/t/	/d/	/əd/
4. shouted	/t/	/d/	/əd/
5. helped	/t/	/d/	/əd/
6. prepared	/t/	/d/	/əd/
7. erased	/t/	/d/	/əd/
8. ended	/t/	/d/	/əd/
9. pointed	/t/	/d/	/əd/

◇ **PRACTICE 37. Verb review: past tense.**

Directions: Complete the sentences. Use the verbs in parentheses.

1. Ann and I *(go)* _____went_____ to the bookstore yesterday. I *(buy)*

   _____ some paperback books and a birthday card.

2. I had to go downtown yesterday. I *(catch)* _____ the bus in front of

   my apartment and *(ride)* _____ to Grand Avenue. Then I *(get off)*

   _____ the bus and transferred to another one. It *(be)*

   _____ a long trip.

3. Sue *(eat)* _____ popcorn and *(drink)* _____ a soft

   drink at the movie theater last night. I *(eat, not)* _____ anything. I'm
   on a diet.

4. Maria *(ask)* _____ the teacher a question in class yesterday. The

   teacher *(think)* _____ about the question for a few minutes and then
   said, "I don't know."

5. I *(want)* _____ *(go)* _____ to the basketball game

   last night, but I *(stay)* _____ home because I had to study.

6. Last night I *(read)* _____ an article in the newspaper. It *(be)*

   _____ about the snowstorm in Moscow.

7. Rita *(pass, not)* _____ the test yesterday. She *(fail)*

   _____ it.

8. Last summer we *(drive)* _____ to

   Colorado for our vacation. We *(visit)* _____

   a national park, where we *(camp)* _____

   in our tent for a week. We *(go)* _____

   fishing one morning. I *(catch)* _____

   a very big fish, but my husband *(catch, not)* _____

   anything. We *(enjoy)* _____ cooking and

   eating the fish for dinner. It *(be)* _____ delicious.
   I like fresh fish.

◇ **PRACTICE 38. Verb review: past and present.**

Directions: Complete the sentences with the *italic* words in parentheses. Use the simple present, present progressive, or simple past. The sentence may require statement, negative, or question forms.

1. Tom *(walk)* _____walks_____ to work almost every day.

2. I can see Tom from my window. He's on the street below. He *(walk)* _____
_____ to work right now.

3. *(Tom, walk)* _____ to work every day?

4. *(you, walk)* _____ to work every day?

5. I usually take the bus to work, but yesterday I *(walk)* _____
to my office.

6. On my way to work yesterday, I *(see)* _____ an accident.

7. Alex *(see, not)* _____ the accident.

8. *(you, see)* _____ the accident yesterday?

9. Tom *(walk, not)* _____ to work last week. The weather
was too cold. He *(take)* _____ the bus.

10. I *(walk, not)* _____ to work last week either.

◇ **PRACTICE 39. Verb review: past and present.**

Directions: Complete the sentences. Use the words in parentheses. Use any appropriate verb form.

1. I *(finish, not)* _____didn't finish_____ my homework last night. I *(go)*
_____ to bed early.

2. Jasmin *(stand, not)* _____ up right now. She *(sit)*
_____ down.

3. The weather *(be, not)* _____ cold today, but it *(be)*
_____ cold yesterday.

4. It *(rain, not)* _____ right now. The rain *(stop)*
_____ a few minutes ago.

5. Tina and I *(go, not)* _____ shopping yesterday. We *(go)*
_____ shopping last Monday.

6. I (go) _____ to a movie last night, but I (enjoy, not)

_____ it. It (be, not) _____ very good.

7. I (write) _____ a letter to my girlfriend yesterday, but I

(write, not) _____ a letter to her last week.

8. My husband (come, not) _____ home for dinner last night.

9. The children (go) _____ to bed a half an hour ago. They (sleep)

_____ now.

10. We (be) _____ late for the movie last night. The movie (start)

_____ at seven, but we (arrive, not) _____

until 7:15.

11. Olga (ask) _____ Hamid a question a few minutes ago, but he

(answer, not) _____ her question.

12. When Ben and I (go) _____ to the department store yesterday, I

(buy) _____ some new socks. Ben (buy, not)

_____ anything.

13. A: What did you do yesterday?

B: Well, I (wake up) _____ around nine and (go)

_____ shopping. While I was downtown, someone (steal)

_____ my purse. I (take) _____ a

taxi home. When I (get) _____ out of the taxi, I (tear)

_____ my blouse. I (borrow) _____

some money from my roommate to pay the taxi driver.

A: Did anything good happen to you yesterday?

B: Hmmm. Let me think. Oh, yes. I (lose) _____ my grammar

book, but I (find) _____ it later.

14. A: May I see the classified section of the newspaper?

B: Sure. Here it is.

A: Thanks. I (want) _____ (look)

_____ at the want ads. I (need)

_____ (find) _____ a new apartment.

APTS., UNFURN.
---
2 BR. $725/mo. Lake St.
Near bus. All utils. incl.
No pets. 361-3663. eves.

APPENDIX 1
Irregular Verbs

SIMPLE FORM	SIMPLE PAST	SIMPLE FORM	SIMPLE PAST
be	was, were	keep	kept
become	became	know	knew
begin	began	leave	left
bend	bent	lend	lent
bite	bit	lose	lost
blow	blew	make	made
break	broke	meet	met
bring	brought	pay	paid
build	built	put	put
buy	bought	read	read
catch	caught	ride	rode
choose	chose	ring	rang
come	came	run	ran
cost	cost	say	said
cut	cut	see	saw
do	did	sell	sold
draw	drew	send	sent
drink	drank	shake	shook
drive	drove	shut	shut
eat	ate	sing	sang
fall	fell	sit	sat
feed	fed	sleep	slept
feel	felt	speak	spoke
fight	fought	spend	spent
find	found	stand	stood
fly	flew	steal	stole
forget	forgot	swim	swam
get	got	take	took
give	gave	teach	taught
go	went	tear	tore
grow	grew	tell	told
hang	hung	think	thought
have	had	throw	threw
hear	heard	understand	understood
hide	hid	wake up	woke up
hit	hit	wear	wore
hold	held	win	won
hurt	hurt	write	wrote

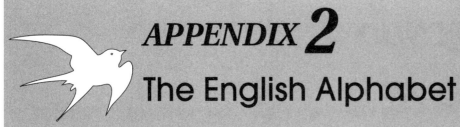

APPENDIX 2
The English Alphabet

A	a	N	n
B	b	O	o
C	c	P	p
D	d	Q	q
E	e	R	r
F	f	S	s
G	g	T	t
H	h	U	u
I	i	V	v
J	j	W	w
K	k	X	x
L	l	Y	y
M	m	Z	z*

Vowels = *a, e, i, o u.*
Consonants = *b, c, d, f, g, h, j, k, l, m, n, p, q, r, s, t, v, w, x, y, z.*

---

*The letter **z** is pronounced "zee" in American English and "zed" in British English.

APPENDIX 3
Numbers

CARDINAL NUMBERS

1	one
2	two
3	three
4	four
5	five
6	six
7	seven
8	eight
9	nine
10	ten
11	eleven
12	twelve
13	thirteen
14	fourteen
15	fifteen
16	sixteen
17	seventeen
18	eighteen
19	nineteen
20	twenty
21	twenty-one
22	twenty-two
23	twenty-three
24	twenty-four
25	twenty-five
26	twenty-six
27	twenty-seven
28	twenty-eight
29	twenty-nine
30	thirty
40	forty
50	fifty
60	sixty
70	seventy
80	eighty
90	ninety
100	one hundred
200	two hundred
1,000	one thousand
10,000	ten thousand
100,000	one hundred thousand
1,000,000	one million

ORDINAL NUMBERS

1st	first
2nd	second
3rd	third
4th	fourth
5th	fifth
6th	sixth
7th	seventh
8th	eighth
9th	ninth
10th	tenth
11th	eleventh
12th	twelfth
13th	thirteenth
14th	fourteenth
15th	fifteenth
16th	sixteenth
17th	seventeenth
18th	eighteenth
19th	nineteenth
20th	twentieth
21st	twenty-first
22nd	twenty-second
23rd	twenty-third
24th	twenty-fourth
25th	twenty-fifth
26th	twenty-sixth
27th	twenty-seventh
28th	twenty-eighth
29th	twenty-ninth
30th	thirtieth
40th	fortieth
50th	fiftieth
60th	sixtieth
70th	seventieth
80th	eightieth
90th	ninetieth
100th	one hundredth
200th	two hundredth

APPENDIX 4
Days of the Week and Months of the Year

DAYS

Monday	(Mon.)
Tuesday	(Tues.)
Wednesday	(Wed.)
Thursday	(Thurs.)
Friday	(Fri.)
Saturday	(Sat.)
Sunday	(Sun.)

MONTHS

January	(Jan.)
February	(Feb.)
March	(Mar.)
April	(Apr.)
May	(May)
June	(June)
July	(July)
August	(Aug.)
September	(Sept.)
October	(Oct.)
November	(Nov.)
December	(Dec.)

Using numbers to write the date:

> month/day/year
> 10/31/41 = October 31, 1941
> 4/15/92 = April 15, 1992
> 7/4/1906 = July 4, 1906
> 7/4/07 = July 4, 2007

Saying dates:

USUAL WRITTEN FORM	USUAL SPOKEN FORM
January 1	January first/the first of January
March 2	March second/the second of March
May 3	May third/the third of May
June 4	June fourth/the fourth of June
August 5	August fifth/the fifth of August
October 10	October tenth/the tenth of October
November 27	November twenty-seventh/the twenty-seventh of November

APPENDIX 5
Ways of Saying Time

9:00	It's nine o'clock. It's nine.
9:05	It's nine-oh-five. It's five (minutes) after nine. It's five (minutes) past nine.
9:10	It's nine-ten. It's ten (minutes) after nine. It's ten (minutes) past nine.
9:15	It's nine-fifteen. It's a quarter after nine. It's a quarter past nine.
9:30	It's nine-thirty. It's half past nine.
9:45	It's nine-forty-five. It's a quarter to ten. It's a quarter of ten.
9:50	It's nine-fifty. It's ten (minutes) to ten. It's ten (minutes) of ten.
12:00	It's noon. It's midnight.

A.M. = morning   It's nine A.M.
P.M. = afternoon/evening/night   It's nine P.M.

APPENDIX 6

Two-Syllable Verbs: Spelling of *-ED* and *-ING*

	VERB	SPEAKING STRESS
(a)	visit	**VIS** · it
(b)	admit	ad · **MIT**

Some verbs have two syllables. In (a): *visit* has two syllables: *vis + it*. In the word *visit*, the stress is on the first syllable. In (b): the stress is on the second syllable in the word *admit*.

	VERB	STRESS	*-ED* FORM	*-ING* FORM
(c)	visit	**VIS** · it	visited	visiting
(d)	open	**O** · pen	opened	opening
(e)	admit	ad · **MIT**	admitted	admitting
(f)	occur	oc · **CUR**	occurred	occurring

For two-syllable verbs that end in a vowel and a consonant:
- The consonant is not doubled if the stress is on the first syllable, as in (c) and (d).
- The consonant is doubled if the stress is on the second syllable, as in (e) and (f).

COMMON VERBS

Stress on first syllable:

VERB	STRESS	*-ED* FORM	*-ING* FORM
answer	**AN** · swer	answered	answering
happen	**HAP** · pen	happened	happening
listen	**LIS** · ten	listened	listening
offer	**OF** · fer	offered	offering
enter	**EN** · ter	entered	entering

Stress on second syllable:

VERB	STRESS	*-ED* FORM	*-ING* FORM
prefer	pre · **FER**	preferred	preferring
permit	per · **MIT**	permitted	permitting
refer	re · **FER**	referred	referring
begin	be · **GIN**	(no *-ed* form)	beginning

Index

◇ PRACTICE 14, p. 6.

	Negative	Contraction
1.	are not	aren't OR you're not
2.	is not	isn't OR she's not
3.	am not	I'm not
4.	is not	isn't OR he's not
5.	is not	isn't
6.	is not	isn't OR it's not
7.	are not	aren't OR we're not
8.	are not	aren't OR you're not
9.	are not	aren't OR they're not

◇ PRACTICE 15, p. 6.

1. aren't   5. are   9. is
2. isn't   6. aren't   10. isn't
3. is   7. is
4. is   8. isn't

◇ PRACTICE 16, p. 7.

1. isn't . . . 's a country
2. aren't . . . 're machines
3. is . . . isn't
4. aren't . . . 're seasons
5. isn't . . . 's a language
6. 'm not . . . 'm a student
7. 're . . . aren't

◇ PRACTICE 17, p. 7.

1. isn't
2. isn't
3. are
4. aren't
5. isn't . . . is
6. is/isn't . . . is/isn't
7. is/isn't . . . is/isn't
8. aren't . . . are
9. is . . . isn't
10. aren't . . . are

◇ PRACTICE 18, p. 8.

1. Apples aren't blue. They're red.
2. A circle is round. It isn't square.
3. A piano is heavy. It isn't light.
4. Potato chips aren't sweet. They're salty.
5. The Sahara Desert is large. It isn't small.
6. The Nile River isn't short. It's long.
7. This exercise is/isn't easy. It is/isn't difficult.
8. My grammar book is/isn't new. It is/isn't old.
9. Electric cars are expensive. They aren't cheap.

◇ PRACTICE 19, p. 8.

1. in . . . in his apartment
2. at . . . at the airport
3. from . . . from Egypt
4. on . . . on my desk
5. in . . . in his pocket
6. on . . . on First Street
7. next to . . . next to the bank
8. under . . . under my desk
9. between . . . between my cheeks
10. on . . . on the third floor / above . . . above Mr. Kwan's apartment

◇ PRACTICE 20, p. 9.

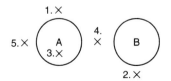

◇ PRACTICE 21, p. 9.

Nouns	Adjectives	Prepositions
city	easy	at
country	empty	between
parents	happy	next to
sister	hungry	on
teacher	single	outside

◇ PRACTICE 22, p. 10

Sample answers:
1. a dentist / a doctor, etc.
   here / at home, etc.
   friendly / nice, etc.
2. a friend.
   at school.
   smart.
3. big.
   in Europe and Asia.
   a country.
4. on my desk.
   helpful.
   a book.

◇ PRACTICE 23, p. 10.

1. Canada isn't a city.
2. Canada is in North America.
3. France is next to Germany.
4. The downstairs of a building is not above the upstairs.
5. Ice isn't hot.
6. Apples and oranges aren't vegetables.
7. Airplanes are fast.
8. Alligators aren't friendly.
9. An alligator is dangerous.
10. Vegetables are healthy.

◇ PRACTICE 24, p. 11.

1. is   5. are
2. is   6. are
3. is   7. is
4. is

◇ PRACTICE 25, p. 11.

1. am   4. am   7. am
2. is   5. is   8. is
3. is   6. is   9. am

Chapter 2: USING *BE* AND *HAVE*

◇ PRACTICE 1, p. 12.

1. Are you a student?
2. Is he a student?
3. Are they teachers?
4. Is she from Canada?
5. Are you ready?
6. Are we ready?
7. Is it ready?

◇ PRACTICE 2, p. 12.

1. Are you a student?
2. Are bananas healthy?
3. Is Ann a doctor?
4. Are the children at school?
5. Are you ready for the test?
6. Is Liz at school?
7. Are you tired?

◇ **PRACTICE 3, p. 13.**
1. it is
2. they are
3. they are
4. he is
5. they are
6. it is
7. she is
8. I am
9. we are
10. you are

◇ **PRACTICE 4, p. 13.**
1. Is . . . is
2. Is . . . is
3. Is . . . is
4. Is . . . is
5. Are . . . are
6. Is . . . is
7. Are . . . are
8. Are . . . are
9. Are . . . am
10. Are . . . are

◇ **PRACTICE 5, p. 14.**
1. Is . . . is
2. Is Dong . . . is
3. Are they . . . they are
4. Is Rosa . . . isn't
5. Is Dong . . . he is
6. Is Rosa . . . she is
7. Is Dong . . . isn't
8. Are they . . . aren't

◇ **PRACTICE 6, p. 14.**
1. A: Is
   B: she is
   A: Are you
2. A: Are you
   B: aren't/'re not . . . 're
   A: he isn't/he's not . . . 's

◇ **PRACTICE 7, p. 15.**
1. b   3. a   5. a
2. b   4. b   6. b

◇ **PRACTICE 8, p. 15.**
1. Where is the teacher?
2. Is the teacher in the classroom?
3. Where are Pablo and Dina?
4. Are Pablo and Dina at home?
5. Is the map in the car?
6. Where is the store?
7. Are you outside?
8. Where are you?

◇ **PRACTICE 9, p. 16.**
1. have   5. has   9. have
2. have   6. has   10. have
3. has   7. has   11. have
4. has   8. has

◇ **PRACTICE 10, p. 16.**
My apartment
1. has   4. is   7. is
2. is   5. has   8. has
3. is   6. is   9. has

My apartment manager
1. is   4. has   7. is
2. has   5. has   8. is
3. is   6. is   9. has

◇ **PRACTICE 11, p. 16.**
1. are . . . have
2. has . . . is
3. am . . . have
4. are . . . have
5. has . . . is

◇ **PRACTICE 12, p. 17.**
1. are   4. have   7. has
2. has   5. has   8. is
3. has   6. have

◇ **PRACTICE 13, p. 17.**
1. His   7. Their
2. Your   8. His
3. My   9. Her
4. Our   10. Their
5. Your   11. Our
6. Their 12. Our

◇ **PRACTICE 14, p. 18.**
1. His   4. Their
2. Their 5. Her
3. His   6. Her

◇ **PRACTICE 15, p. 19.**
1. have . . . My
2. have . . . Their
3. have . . . Your
4. have . . . Our
5. has . . . His
6. has . . . Her
7. has . . . His
8. have . . . Their
9. have . . . My
10. have . . . Their

◇ **PRACTICE 16, p. 19.**
1. This   5. This
2. That   6. That
3. That   7. This
4. This   8. That

◇ **PRACTICE 17, p. 20.**
1. These   4. Those
2. These   5. These
3. Those   6. Those

◇ **PRACTICE 18, p. 20.**
1. This . . . Those
2. These . . . Those
3. This . . . That
4. These . . . That
5. This . . . That
6. These . . . Those
7. This . . . Those

◇ **PRACTICE 19, p. 21.**
1. a   4. a
2. a   5. b
3. b   6. b

◇ **PRACTICE 20, p. 21.**
1. Who is that?
2. What is that?
3. What are those?
4. Who are they?
5. What are those?
6. Who is that?

◇ **PRACTICE 21, p. 22.**
1. Yes, they are.
2. This is Donna.
3. Yes, it is.
4. Yes, she is.
5. No, it isn't.
6. Yes, he is.
7. It's in Norway.
8. Yes, I am.
9. This is an insect.

◇ PRACTICE 22, p. 22.

1. her   4. their
2. Their   5. His
3. her

◇ PRACTICE 23, p. 23.

1. have   6. is   11. is
2. is   7. is   12. am
3. has   8. has   13. am
4. is   9. is   14. have
5. is   10. is   15. are

Chapter 3: USING THE SIMPLE PRESENT

◇ PRACTICE 1, p. 24.

1. walk   5. walk   9. walk
2. walk   6. walks   10. walks
3. walk   7. walks   11. walks
4. walks   8. walks   12. walk

◇ PRACTICE 2, p. 24.

Spiro <u>works</u> at night. He <u>teaches</u> auto mechanics at a school in his town. He <u>leaves</u> his apartment at 5:00. He <u>catches</u> the bus near his home. The bus <u>comes</u> at 5:15. It <u>takes</u> him 40 minutes to get to work. His classes <u>begin</u> at 6:30. He <u>teaches</u> until 10:30. He <u>stays</u> at school until 11:15. A friend <u>drives</u> him home. He <u>gets</u> home around midnight.

◇ PRACTICE 3, p. 25.

1. rings   7. discuss
2. get   8. work
3. makes   9. arrive
4. cooks   10. come
5. leave   11. take
6. bring

◇ PRACTICE 4, p. 25.

1. wakes   7. cooks
2. wake   8. falls
3. eat   9. eat
4. eats   10. fall
5. leaves   11. see
6. take   12. have

◇ PRACTICE 5, p. 26.

1. Olga always has cream in her coffee.
2. I rarely eat breakfast.
3. The students seldom buy their lunch at school.
4. They usually bring a lunch from home.
5. My husband and I often go out to a restaurant for dinner.
6. My husband sometimes drinks tea with dinner.
7. We never have dessert.

◇ PRACTICE 6, p. 26.

1. Beth sometimes has fish for lunch.
2. Roger rarely/seldom gets up late.
3. Mr. and Mrs. Phillips usually go to the movies on weekends.
4. I often clean my apartment.

5. My roommate never cleans our apartment.
6. The students always do their homework.
7. The teacher sometimes corrects papers on weekends.

◇ PRACTICE 7, p. 27.

Free response.

◇ PRACTICE 8, p. 27.

Free response.

◇ PRACTICE 9, p. 28.

1. I have classes three times a week.
2. I exercise once a day.
3. I pay my phone bill once a month.
4. I visit my cousins twice a year.
5. Dr. Williams checks her e-mail three times a day.
6. The Browns take a long vacation once a year.
7. Cyndi gives dinner parties twice a month.
8. Sam buys vegetables at the farmers' market twice a week.

◇ PRACTICE 10, p. 29.

1. Joan is often sick.   6. am usually
2. often feels   7. usually go
3. is sometimes   8. never sleep
4. is rarely   9. never wake up
5. rarely rains   10. am always

◇ PRACTICE 11, p. 29.

1. The teacher usually cleans up the classroom
2. The students often help the teacher.
3. The classroom is always clean.
4. The parents frequently visit the class.
5. The parents sometimes help the students with their work.
6. The parents are always helpful.

◇ PRACTICE 12, p. 30.

-s	-es
eats	catches
talks	finishes
sleeps	fixes
listens	wishes
calls	kisses

◇ PRACTICE 13, p. 30.

1. teach   9. wash
2. teaches   10. washes
3. mix   11. cooks
4. mixes   12. reads
5. misses   13. watches
6. miss   14. begins
7. brush   15. come
8. brushes   16. comes

◇ PRACTICE 14, p. 31.

1. study   6. study
2. studies   7. studies
3. study   8. study
4. studies   9. studies
5. study   10. study

◇ PRACTICE 15, p. 31.

-*ies*	-*s*
tries	pays
worries	buys
flies	enjoys
cries	plays
studies	says

◇ PRACTICE 16, p. 32.

1. starts
2. brushes
3. closes
4. fly
5. flies
6. stops
7. fixes
8. call . . . calls
9. studies
10. helps

◇ PRACTICE 17, p. 32.

1. a. has class at 9:00.
   b. does homework at 10:00.
   c. goes to work at 11:00.
2. a. has class at 10:00.
   b. does homework at 11:00.
   c. goes to work at 2:00.
3. a. do homework at 9:00.
   b. have class at 11:00.
   c. go to work at 1:00.

◇ PRACTICE 18, p. 33.

1. leaves
2. catches
3. gets
4. works
5. fixes
6. come
7. finishes
8. often meets
9. helps
10. usually have
11. goes
12. has
13. is
14. enjoys

◇ PRACTICE 19, p. 34.

PART B.

7. claps /s/
8. bites /s/
9. gets /s/
10. asks /s/
11. talks /s/
12. coughs /s/

◇ PRACTICE 20, p. 35.

PART B.

8. stands /z/
9. lives /z/
10. smiles /z/
11. comes /z/
12. rains /z/
13. remembers /z/
14. snows /z/

◇ PRACTICE 21, p. 35.

1. brushes
2. catches
3. fixes
4. misses
5. teaches
6. kisses

◇ PRACTICE 22, p. 36.

1. fixes /əz/
2. likes /s/
3. sleeps /s/
4. runs /z/
5. writes /s/
6. wears /z/
7. thinks /s/
8. drives /z/
9. misses /əz/
10. helps /s/

◇ PRACTICE 23, p. 36.

	have	*eat*	*be*
1.	don't have	don't eat	am not
2.	don't have	don't eat	aren't
3.	doesn't have	doesn't eat	isn't
4.	doesn't have	doesn't eat	isn't
5.	doesn't have	doesn't eat	isn't
6.	don't have	don't eat	aren't
7.	don't have	don't eat	aren't

◇ PRACTICE 24, p. 36.

1. I don't have time.
2. You don't need more time.
3. They don't eat breakfast.
4. Yoshi doesn't like bananas.
5. Susan doesn't do her homework.
6. We don't walk to school.
7. The phone doesn't work.

◇ PRACTICE 25, p. 37.

1. don't wear
2. is
3. doesn't have
4. breaks
5. don't grow
6. doesn't walk
7. don't fly
8. don't have
9. helps
10. doesn't fix
11. fixes
12. don't like
13. chase

◇ PRACTICE 26, p. 38.

1. Tom and Janet drink coffee.
2. Mark watches TV.
3. Tom walks to school.
4. Tom, Janet, and Mark study grammar.
5. Janet goes shopping.
6. Tom doesn't take the bus.
7. Tom and Janet don't watch TV.
8. Mark doesn't skip lunch.
9. Janet doesn't eat dinner at home.
10. Tom and Mark don't eat dinner out.

◇ PRACTICE 27, p. 39.

1. likes . . . doesn't like
2. knows . . . doesn't know
3. want . . . don't want
4. isn't . . . doesn't want
5. doesn't drink . . . drinks
6. am not . . . don't have
7. doesn't belong . . . belongs
8. don't live . . . have
9. is . . . isn't . . . don't need
10. is . . . don't have
11. doesn't eat . . . isn't
12. read . . . don't watch
13. doesn't read . . . watches

◇ PRACTICE 28, p. 40.

1. Does she study?
2. Do they study?
3. Does he know?
4. Does the doctor know?
5. Do we know?
6. Do I understand?

7. Do you understand?
8. Do the students understand?
9. Does your roommate work?
10. Does the car work?
11. Does it work?
12. Do I work?

◇ PRACTICE 29, p. 40.
1. a. Does he swim?
   b. Does he play soccer?
   c. Does he run?
   d. Does he lift weights?
2. a. Does he run?
   b. Does he swim? OR Does he play soccer?
   c. Does he lift weights?
3. a. Do they play soccer?
   b.–c. Do they swim? OR Do they run? OR Do they lift weights?

◇ PRACTICE 30, p. 41.
1. A   4. B   7. A
2. A   5. A   8. B
3. B   6. B

◇ PRACTICE 31, p. 41.
1. Does she examine . . . she doesn't
2. Does he fix . . . he doesn't
3. Do you fly . . . I don't
4. Do you teach . . . we don't
5. Do they design . . . they don't
6. Do you clean . . . we don't
7. Is she a writer . . . she isn't
8. Are you a nurse . . . I'm not
9. Are they construction workers . . . they aren't
10. Is he a musician . . . he isn't

◇ PRACTICE 32, p. 42.
Sentences that answer "where": 1, 3, 6, 7

◇ PRACTICE 33, p. 43.
1. Where does Paulo spend most of his time?
2. Where does he work in the summer?
3. Where does he stay (in the summer)?
4. Where does he work in the winter?
5. Where does he live (in the winter)?

◇ PRACTICE 34, p. 43.
1. Where does David live?
2. Where is the teacher?
3. Where does Dr. Varma stay?
4. Does she stay at the Plaza Hotel?
5. Where do you catch the bus?
6. Do you catch the bus on First Street?
7. Where do the construction workers eat lunch?
8. Is your mother outside?
9. Where is she?

◇ PRACTICE 35, p. 44.
1. Where   6. When
2. When   7. Where
3. When   8. When
4. Where   9. When
5. Where   10. Where

◇ PRACTICE 36, p. 44.
1. When do you go to bed?
2. Do you get up early?
3. When does the bus come?
4. Does the bus come on time?
5. Where do you work?
6. When do you start work?
7. When do you leave work?
8. Do you like your job?
9. Is it interesting work?

◇ PRACTICE 37, p. 45.
1. Is he a teacher? Yes, he is.
2. What does he teach? He teaches biology and chemistry.
3. Where does he teach chemistry? He teaches chemistry in the chemistry lab.
4. When is he in the chemistry lab? He is in the chemistry lab at 12:00.
5. Where does he teach biology? He teaches biology in the biology lab.
6. Is he in his office every day? No, he isn't.
7. Is he in his office at 1:00? Yes, he is.
8. Does he teach at 8:00? No, he doesn't
9. When does he teach? He teaches at 9:00, 10:00, and 12:00.

◇ PRACTICE 38, p. 46.
1. Are   5. Is   9. Do
2. Is   6. Do   10. Are
3. Does   7. Do
4. Do   8. Do

◇ PRACTICE 39, p. 46.
1. A: Are   4. A: Are
   B: am   A: Are
   A: Are   A: are
   B: am   B: are
   A: Do   5. A: Is
   B: don't   B: isn't
2. A: Do   A: is
   B: do . . . is   A: Is
3. A: Are   B: isn't
   B: am   A: is
   A: Do   6. A: are . . . Do
   A: Do   B: Are
   B: don't   A: aren't
                    B: Are
                    B: are

◇ PRACTICE 40, p. 47.
1. isn't   7. costs
2. loves   8. know
3. studies   9. don't want
4. don't have   10. A: look
5. doesn't clean   B: am not
6. tastes

◇ PRACTICE 41, p. 48.
1. Is Jane at home?
2. Where is she?
3. Are Susie and Johnny at home?
4. Where are they?
5. When is dinner?
6. What does Jane have in the fridge?

◇ **PRACTICE 42, p. 48.**
1. enjoys
2. makes
3. like Ø
4. invite Ø
5. go Ø
6. watch Ø
7. watches
8. makes
9. washes
10. cleans
11. cooks
12. knows

◇ **PRACTICE 43, p. 49.**
1. B
2. B
3. A
4. C
5. C
6. C
7. A
8. B
9. B
10. C

Chapter 4: USING THE PRESENT PROGRESSIVE

◇ **PRACTICE 1, p. 50.**
1. are
2. is
3. am
4. is
5. is
6. are
7. is
8. is
9. are
10. are
11. is
12. are
13. are
14. are

◇ **PRACTICE 2, p. 50.**
1. shining
2. winning
3. joining
4. signing
5. flying
6. paying
7. studying
8. getting
9. waiting
10. writing

◇ **PRACTICE 3, p. 51.**
1. dreaming
2. coming
3. looking
4. taking
5. biting
6. hitting
7. hurting
8. clapping
9. keeping
10. camping

◇ **PRACTICE 4, p. 51.**
1. are waiting
2. are sitting
3. are talking
4. is doing
5. is reading
6. are kicking
7. is coming
8. are going

◇ **PRACTICE 5, p. 52.**
PART A.
1. He is meeting with his manager.
2. He isn't repairing his car.
3. He is working at his computer.
4. He is talking on the phone.
5. He isn't riding a horse.
6. He isn't buying food for dinner.

PART B.
1. They are talking to patients.
2. They aren't washing cars.
3. They aren't watching movies.
4. They are working with doctors.
5. They are giving medicine to patients.

PART C.
Free response.

◇ **PRACTICE 6, p. 53.**
Answers will vary.
1. am/am not thinking
2. am/am not writing
3. am/am not going
4. am/am not traveling
5. is/is not sitting
6. is/is not singing
7. is/is not ringing
8. is/is not making

◇ **PRACTICE 7, p. 53.**
1. Is he studying English?
2. Are you working?
3. Are they leaving?
4. Is she staying home?
5. Are we going to school?
6. Is the computer working?
7. Is it working?
8. Am I driving?
9. Is your friend coming?
10. Are the students laughing?
11. Is Mr. Kim sleeping?
12. Is Monica dreaming?

◇ **PRACTICE 8, p. 54.**
1. A: Is she sleeping?
   B: she isn't . . . is cooking
2. A: Is he running?
   B: he isn't . . . is driving
3. A: Are they studying?
   B: they aren't . . . are swimming
4. A: Is she teaching?
   B: isn't . . . is shopping
5. A: Are they cleaning?
   B: aren't . . . are hiking
6. A: Is she fishing?
   B: isn't . . . is sleeping
7. A: Are they working?
   B: they aren't . . . are playing
8. A: Are you riding a bike?
   B: I'm not . . . am sitting

◇ **PRACTICE 9, p. 55.**
1. every day
2. now
3. every day
4. every day
5. now
6. now
7. every day
8. now
9. now
10. every day

◇ **PRACTICE 10, p. 55.**
Checked sentences: 1, 2, 6, 8, 9

◇ **PRACTICE 11, p. 55.**
1. is shining
2. am looking
3. are fishing
4. is sitting
5. are playing
6. are swimming
7. are jumping
8. swim
9. walk
10. go
11. am working
12. work
13. write
14. am writing

◇ PRACTICE 12, p. 56.

1. Do
2. Are
3. Is
4. Are
5. Do
6. Is
7. Does
8. Do
9. Does
10. Do
11. Does
12. Do
13. Are
14. Do

◇ PRACTICE 13, p. 56.

1. Do you know
2. smell
3. is crying . . . wants
4. tastes . . . like
5. are running . . . likes . . . hates

◇ PRACTICE 14, p. 57.

1. A: tastes
   B: think
2. A: does Jan want
   B: needs . . . wants
3. A: Do you hear
   B: hear . . . don't see
4. A: loves
   B: don't believe . . . loves

◇ PRACTICE 15, p. 57.

1. b
2. a
3. a
4. a
5. b
6. a
7. a
8. b
9. a

◇ PRACTICE 16, p. 58.

1. is watching
2. is playing
3. is also listening
4. (is) looking
5. is wearing
6. is talking
7. is telling
8. isn't listening
9. doesn't hear
10. is listening

◇ PRACTICE 17, p. 58.

1. watch
2. hear
3. hear
4. listen to
5. A: look at
   B: look at . . . watch
6. A: Do you see
   B: see

◇ PRACTICE 18, p. 58.

Sample answers:
1. am writing in my book.
2. see a window.
3. hear music.
4. am listening to music.
5. am watching a bird outside.
6. want lunch.
7. need money.

◇ PRACTICE 19, p. 59.

1. b
2. a
3. b
4. a
5. a

◇ PRACTICE 20, p. 59.

1. A: are . . . thinking about
   B: am thinking about
   A: think

2. A: think
   B: do . . . think . . . think
3. A: am thinking about
   B: Are . . . thinking about
   B: think
   A: think

◇ PRACTICE 21, p. 60.

1. eats . . . rings . . . doesn't answer . . . doesn't want . . . believes
2. flies . . . is flying
3. is taking
4. A: Are you waiting
   B: am
   A: does the bus stop
   A: Is it usually
   B: It rarely comes
5. A: does your teacher usually do
   B: think . . . corrects . . . has
   A: is she doing
   B: is talking
6. A: Do you know
   B: believe . . . is
   B: know

Chapter 5: TALKING ABOUT THE PRESENT

◇ PRACTICE 1, p. 61.

1. What day is it?
2. What time is it?
3. What's the date today?
4. What year is it?
5. What month is it?
6. What time is it?
7. What's the date today?

◇ PRACTICE 2, p. 61.

1. A
2. B
3. B
4. A
5. B

◇ PRACTICE 3, p. 62.

1. a. in
   b. at
2. a. at
   b. in
   c. on
3. a. in
   b. at
   c. from . . . to
   d. at
   e. on
   f. on
4. a. in
   b. on
   c. in
   d. at . . . in
   e. on
   f in

◇ PRACTICE 4, p. 63.

1. in
2. at
3. from . . . to
4. on
5. in
6. at
7. in
8. on
9. from . . . to

◇ PRACTICE 5, p. 63.

PART A.
1. How's the weather / What's the weather like in Cairo?
2. How's the weather / What's the weather like in Sydney?
3. How's the weather / What's the weather like in Seoul?
4. How's the weather / What's the weather like in Sydney?
5. How's the weather / What's the weather like in Moscow?

PART B.
6. yes   8. no   10. yes
7. no   9. no   11. no

◇ PRACTICE 6, p. 64.
1. B   4. A   6. B
2. A   5. A   7. A
3. B

◇ PRACTICE 7, p. 64.
1. is . . . yes   4. is   7. is
2. are   5. are   8. is
3. is   6. are   9. are

◇ PRACTICE 8, p. 65.
1. There are two chairs.
2. There is one sofa.
3. There is one table.
4. There are four books.
5. There is one lamp.
6. There are two pillows.

◇ PRACTICE 9, p. 65.
1. Is   4. Is   7. Is
2. Is   5. Are   8. Are
3. Are   6. Are   9. Is

◇ PRACTICE 10, p. 66.
1. Is there a subway?
2. Is there a bus station?
3. Are there fast-food restaurants?
4. Are there movie theaters?
5. Is there a park?
6. Are there places to go running?
7. Is there a visitor information office?

◇ PRACTICE 11, p. 66.
1. boys   5. minutes
2. girls   6. seconds
3. cars   7. stars
4. words   8. snowflakes

◇ PRACTICE 12, p. 67.
1. How many continents are there
2. How many states are there
3. How many colors are there
4. How many countries are there
5. How many letters are there
6. How many main languages are there

◇ PRACTICE 13, p. 67.
1. How many sentences are there is this exercise? There are seven.
2. How many exercises are there in this chapter? There are 23.

3. How many pages are there in your dictionary? There are . . .
4. How many students are there in your class? There are . . .
5. How many males are there in your class? There are . . .
6. How many females are there in your class? There are . . .
7. How many teachers are there at your school? There are . . .

◇ PRACTICE 14, p. 68.
1. in   4. at   7. on
2. in   5. on   8. at
3. on   6. in

◇ PRACTICE 15, p. 68.
1. in/inside
2. in front of
3. behind/in back of
4. on/on top of
5. next to/beside/near
6. above
7. under
8. between

◇ PRACTICE 16, p. 69.
Sample answers:
1. Under my desk. / On the floor / Etc.
2. On the floor.
3. On my desk.
4. On my book.
5. On my desk.
6. In my hand.

◇ PRACTICE 17, p. 70.

need	*want*
air	a camera phone
electricity	diamond jewelry
food	a DVD player
money	an expensive house
a place to live	a leather coat
water	a sports car

◇ PRACTICE 18, p. 70.
1. to   4. to   7. to
2. Ø   5. to   8. Ø
3. Ø   6. Ø

◇ PRACTICE 19, p. 71.
1. The children need a snack.
2. They want to have potato chips and soda.
3. Their mother wants to give them apples and oranges.
4. The children don't want to eat fruit.
5. They want junk food.
6. They need to eat healthy food.

◇ PRACTICE 20, p. 71.
1. would like   7. would like
2. would like   8. would like
3. would like   9. would like
4. would like   10. would like
5. would like   11. would like
6. would like   12. would like

◇ PRACTICE 21, p. 72.
1. want 4. wants
2. like 5. like
3. likes 6. want

◇ PRACTICE 22, p. 72.
1. Mark would like to have a large family.
2. *(no change)*
3. *(no change)*
4. Mark would like to get married this year.
5. He would like a pet this year, too.
6. *(no change)*
7. What would he like first?

◇ PRACTICE 23, p. 73.
1. B 5. D 9. B
2. A 6. D 10. D
3. A 7. A
4. C 8. B

Chapter 6: NOUNS AND PRONOUNS

◇ PRACTICE 1, p. 74.
Nouns: 1, 5, 6, 7, 8, 9

◇ PRACTICE 2, p. 74.
Nouns: store, list, eggs, bananas, rice, tea, cell, Judy

◇ PRACTICE 3, p. 75.
Subjects:
1. The weather 4. The children . . . their parents
2. Snow 5. Some people
3. The sun 6. Teenagers

◇ PRACTICE 4, p. 75.
	Completions	*Objects*
1.	Worms.	worms
2.	No.	Ø *(no object)*
3.	Patients.	patients
4.	Milk.	milk
5.	No.	Ø *(no object)*
6.	Their mothers.	their mothers

◇ PRACTICE 5, p. 75.
Objects:
1. a. the newspaper 5. b. lunch
   c. the newspaper 6. a. English
2. c. soccer d. English
3. b. eggs 7. *(no object)*
   c. eggs 8. b. Maria
4. a. bones
   b. furniture

◇ PRACTICE 6, p. 76.
Checked sentences; objects of prepositions:
2. morning 7. street
3. children 9. work
4. table 10. house

◇ PRACTICE 7, p. 76.
Checked sentences; objects of prepositions:
1. a. bakery 3. b. library
2. a. backpack d. night
   c. snack 4. a. students
   c. classroom

◇ PRACTICE 8, p. 77.
Nouns	*Adjectives*
food	fresh
car	poor
leg	bright
tree	easy
test	nervous
rain	quiet
chair	wet

◇ PRACTICE 9, p. 77.
1. sad 6. interesting
2. old 7. slow
3. hard 8. short
4. ugly 9. difficult, hard
5. old 10. quiet

◇ PRACTICE 10, p. 78.
1. My sister lives in a new apartment. *(N ... A N)*
2. It is very bright. *(A)*
3. The rooms are large and have tall ceilings. *(N ... A ... A N)*
4. Her building is next to a Japanese restaurant. *(N ... A N)*
5. I love food from other countries. *(N ... N)*
6. Mexican food is spicy and delicious. *(A N A ... A)*
7. There is a wonderful café in my neighborhood. *(A N ... N)*
8. My neighbors like to meet there for coffee. *(N ... N)*

◇ PRACTICE 11, p. 78.
Sample answers:
1. smart, new, old, happy
2. hard, easy, difficult
3. friendly, helpful
4. delicious, fresh, organic, good, bad

◇ PRACTICE 12, p. 78.
1. the United States (of America) 8. Italy
2. Australia 9. Japan
3. Canada 10. Korea
4. China 11. Malaysia
5. Egypt 12. Mexico
6. India 13. Russia
7. Indonesia 14. Saudi Arabia

◇ PRACTICE 13, p. 79.

Free response.

◇ PRACTICE 14, p. 79.

1. She . . . him
2. He . . . her
3. She . . . them
4. He . . . them
5. They . . . them
6. They . . . him
7. They . . . her
8. They . . . them
9. They . . . them

◇ PRACTICE 15, p. 80.

1. him	6. us	11. they
2. her	7. him*	12. he
3. them	8. her*	13. you
4. him	9. she	14. you
5. me	10. he*	

◇ PRACTICE 16, p. 81.

1. them	4. him	7. it
2. it	5. them	8. her
3. them	6. them	9. him

◇ PRACTICE 17, p. 81.

1. B	4. B
2. A	5. A
3. B	

◇ PRACTICE 18, p. 82.

1. They . . . They . . . them
2. They . . . them . . . They . . . it
3. A: her
   B: She . . . her
4. B: I . . . me
   A: he

◇ PRACTICE 19, p. 82.

1. My . . . me
2. Your . . . you
3. Her . . . her
4. His . . . him
5. Our . . . us
6. Their . . . them
7. Her . . . her OR Its . . . it
8. His . . . him OR Its . . . it
9. Its . . . it

◇ PRACTICE 20, p. 83.

1. My		5. you
2. me		6. Our . . . our
3. him . . . his		7. Its
4. it		8. their

---

*Male and female pronouns are commonly used with pets, especially if you know the pet's name.

◇ PRACTICE 21, p. 83.

1. He . . . His . . . him
2. their . . . They . . .
   them . . . their
3. She . . . Her . . . her
4. their . . . Their . . . their
5. I . . . our . . . our . . . us

◇ PRACTICE 22, p. 84.

1. box		6. keys
2. tomatoes		7. city
3. zoos		8. wife
4. pen		9. dishes
5. babies		10. thieves

◇ PRACTICE 23, p. 84.

-s	*-ies*
girls	ladies
coins	cities
trays	parties
shoes	babies

-ves	*-es*
wives	glasses
lives	potatoes
leaves	bushes
thieves	taxes

◇ PRACTICE 24, p. 85.

/s/	/z/	/əz/
hats	boys	wishes
cups	seas	places
books	papers	faces

◇ PRACTICE 25, p. 85.

1. Potatoes /z/	10. cats /s/
2. keys /z/	11. matches /əz/
3. classes /əz/	12. textbooks /s/
4. thieves /z/	13. dictionaries /z/
5. tests /s/	14. lives /z/
6. Babies /z/	15. tops /s/
7. boxes /əz/	16. leaves /z/
8. radios /z/	17. sandwiches /əz/
9. parties /z/	

◇ PRACTICE 26, p. 86.

1. teeth	5. feet
2. mice	6. men
3. sheep	7. children
4. fish	8. women

◇ PRACTICE 27, p. 86.

1. I **work** in my home office in the morning.
2. *(correct)*
3. My father **works** in the library.
4. **He** is a teacher.
5. My mother **is** a professor.
6. **She** is an excellent professor.
7. *(correct)*
8. The university **has** many interesting and useful classes.
9. *(correct)*

◇ PRACTICE 28, p. 87.

1. C	5. D	9. A
2. B	6. A	10. D
3. A	7. B	
4. D	8. C	

Chapter 7: COUNT AND NONCOUNT NOUNS

◇ PRACTICE 1, p. 88.

1. S	4. S	7. P
2. P	5. P	8. S
3. S	6. S	

◇ PRACTICE 2, p. 88.
1. some, a lot of, five, sixty
2. one, a
3. some, a lot of, five, sixty
4. one, a
5. some, a lot of, five, sixty

◇ PRACTICE 3, p. 88.

1. C	4. NC	7. NC
2. C	5. C	8. C
3. NC	6. NC	

◇ PRACTICE 4, p. 89.
1. a, one
2. some, a lot of, ten, twenty
3. some, a lot of
4. some, a lot of
5. some, a lot of, ten, twenty
6. a, one
7. some, a lot of, ten, twenty
8. some, a lot of

◇ PRACTICE 5, p. 89.
1. one book Ø, two books, several books, some books
2. a job Ø, one job Ø, five jobs, a lot of jobs
3. information Ø, some information Ø, a lot of information Ø
4. a fact Ø, two facts, several facts, a lot of facts

◇ PRACTICE 6, p. 89.
1. some, a lot of
2. a, one
3. some, a lot of
4. a, one
5. a, one
6. some, a lot of
7. some, a lot of
8. a, one
9. some, a lot of
10. some, a lot of

◇ PRACTICE 7, p. 90.

1. work	6. advice	
2. homework	7. furniture	
3. music	8. fruit	
4. vocabulary	9. money	
5. information	10. jewelry	

◇ PRACTICE 8, p. 90.

1. money	10. feet	
2. horses	11. fruit	
3. cities	12. potatoes	
4. countries	13. weather	
5. monkeys	14. work	
6. traffic	15. advice	
7. help	16. men	
8. children	17. sentences	
9. furniture		

◇ PRACTICE 9, p. 91.

1. an	6. an	
2. an	7. an	
3. an	8. a	
4. a	9. a	
5. an	10. an	

◇ PRACTICE 10, p. 91.

1. Ø	6. an	
2. a	7. an	
3. Ø	8. Ø	
4. an	9. Ø	
5. a	10. Ø	

◇ PRACTICE 11, p. 92.

1. a	8. an . . . an	
2. a	9. Ø	
3. Ø	10. a	
4. an	11. Ø	
5. Ø	12. an	
6. A	13. an	
7. a	14. an . . . a	

◇ PRACTICE 12, p. 93.

a	*an*	*some*
suggestion	umbrella	advice
dog	elevator	furniture
flower	earache	eggs
letter		gardens
		packages
		mail
		umbrellas

◇ PRACTICE 13, p. 93.

1. a	6. Some	
2. some	7. a	
3. Some	8. some	
4. a	9. some	
5. an	10. an	

◇ PRACTICE 14, p. 93.
1. I have **a** job.
2. I would like **an** interesting job.
3. Tom enjoys his **work**. *(2nd sentence correct)*
4. Let's listen to ~~a~~ music. *(also possible: some music)*
5. *(correct)*
6. Our teacher knows a lot of **facts**.
7. The students want to learn more English **vocabulary**.
8. *(correct)*

◇ **PRACTICE 15, p. 94.**
1. a bag of rice
2. a tube of toothpaste
3. a bar of soap
4. a bunch of bananas
5. a carton of milk
6. a jar of pickles
7. a box of candy
8. a bottle of olive oil
9. a can of corn

◇ **PRACTICE 16, p. 95.**
1. paper
2. lettuce
3. rice, cereal, paper
4. bread, paper, lettuce, cheese
5. bread
6. bananas, lettuce
7. rice, ice cream, cereal
8. water
9. mayonnaise

◇ **PRACTICE 17, p. 95.**
1. a. a
   b. some
   c. some
   d. some
   e. an
   f. a
   g. some
   h. some
2. a. some
   b. a
   c. some
   d. a
   e. a
   f. some
   g. some
   h. some

◇ **PRACTICE 18, p. 96.**
1. much
2. many
3. much
4. much
5. much
6. much
7. much
8. much
9. many
10. many

◇ **PRACTICE 19, p. 96.**
1. a little
2. a few
3. a few
4. a little
5. a little
6. a few
7. a few
8. a few
9. a little
10. a few

◇ **PRACTICE 20, p. 96.**
1. a little information Ø
2. many questions
3. a few . . . pens
4. a few minutes
5. much coffee Ø . . . a little tea Ø
6. many . . . flowers
7. a few flowers . . . many vegetables

◇ **PRACTICE 21, p. 97.**
1. How much cheese do we need?
2. How much olive oil do we need?
3. How many eggs do we need?
4. How much fruit do we need?
5. How many carrots do we need?
6. How much flour do we need?

◇ **PRACTICE 22, p. 97.**
1. a. the
   b. the
   c. the
   d. The
   e. The
2. a. The . . . the
   b. The . . . the
   c. The
   d. The . . . the
   e. The
3. a. the . . . the
   b. The . . . the
   c. The . . . the
   d. The . . . the

◇ **PRACTICE 23, p. 98.**
1. The . . . the
2. The
3. a . . . The . . . the
4. a . . . The . . . the
5. a . . . a . . . a . . . The . . . the
6. a . . . The

◇ **PRACTICE 24, p. 98.**
1. general
2. specific
3. general
4. general
5. specific
6. specific
7. general
8. specific

◇ **PRACTICE 25, p. 99.**
1. Ø
2. The
3. Ø
4. a
5. an
6. Ø
7. an
8. Ø
9. Ø, Ø
10. Ø, Ø, a
11. The . . . the
12. Ø, a

◇ **PRACTICE 26, p. 99.**
1. A
2. B
3. B
4. A
5. A
6. B
7. B
8. A
9. A

◇ **PRACTICE 27, p. 100.**
1. some
2. any
3. some
4. any
5. some/any
6. any
7. some
8. some
9. some/any
10. Some

◇ **PRACTICE 28, p. 100.**
Possible answers:
1. *I need*
   some eggs
   some rice
   some fish
   some flour
   some potatoes
   some apples
   some bananas
   some coffee
   some toothpaste
   some soap
   some oranges
   some soup
   some fruit
   some vegetables
   some meat
2. *I don't need*
   any eggs
   any rice
   any fish
   any flour
   any potatoes
   any apples
   any bananas
   any coffee
   any toothpaste
   any soap
   any oranges
   any soup
   any fruit
   any vegetables
   any meat

◇ PRACTICE 29, p. 101.

1. Korea and Japan are **countries** in Asia.
2. Is there **much traffic** at 5:00 P.M.?
3. Are you ~~a~~ hungry? Could I get you some food?
4. My children come home with a lot of **homework**.
5. ~~The~~ Digital cameras take wonderful pictures.
6. My eggs and coffee don't taste very good. **The** eggs are very salty, and **the** coffee is weak.
7. What do you like better for a snack: **an** orange/orange**s** or ~~the~~ orange juice?
8. I buy ~~the~~ jeans every year.
9. I'm going to **the** bank. I need money.
10. We need to get **some** furniture. Do you know **a** good furniture store?

Chapter 8: EXPRESSING PAST TIME, PART 1

◇ PRACTICE 1, p. 102.

1. was	5. was	9. was
2. were	6. was	10. were
3. was	7. were	
4. were	8. were	

◇ PRACTICE 2, p. 102.

1. were	4. was	7. was
2. were	5. was	8. were
3. was	6. was	9. was

◇ PRACTICE 3, p. 103.

1. wasn't	7. wasn't
2. weren't	8. weren't
3. weren't	9. wasn't
4. weren't	10. weren't
5. wasn't	11. weren't
6. wasn't	

◇ PRACTICE 4, p. 103.

1. wasn't	6. weren't
2. weren't	7. weren't
3. wasn't	8. wasn't
4. weren't	9. wasn't
5. wasn't	

◇ PRACTICE 5, p. 104.

Some possible answers:
1. Mike wasn't out of town yesterday. He was at work.
2. Ricardo wasn't at school. He was on vacation.
3. Lori wasn't at work. She was out of town.
4. Lori and Eva weren't at work. They were out of town.

◇ PRACTICE 6, p. 104.

Free response.

◇ PRACTICE 7, p. 104.

1. Were	6. Was
2. Was	7. Was
3. Was	8. Was
4. Were	9. Were
5. Were	10. Were

◇ PRACTICE 8, p. 105.

1. Were Jake and Kevin at a movie theater? No, they weren't.
   Where were they? They were at the grocery store.
2. Was Ellen at the library? No, she wasn't.
   Where was she? She was at the mall.
3. Were you at a party? No, I wasn't.
   Where were you? I was at home.
4. Was Thomas at the airport? No, he wasn't.
   Where was he? He was at the train station
5. Were your children at school? No, they weren't.
   Where were they? They were at the zoo.
6. Were Liz and you at the park? No, we weren't.
   Where were you? We were at the library.

◇ PRACTICE 9, p. 106.

1. Was	5. Was
2. Were	6. Was
3. Were	7. Were
4. Was	8. Were

◇ PRACTICE 10, p. 106.

1. studied	7. talked
2. studied	8. helped
3. walked	9. helped
4. worked	10. listened
5. smiled	11. listened
6. smiled	

◇ PRACTICE 11, p. 107.

1. watched TV.
2. exercised at a gym.
3. cooked breakfast.
4. talked to friends on the phone.
5. watched TV.

◇ PRACTICE 12, p. 108.

GROUP A.

1. watched	8. finished
2. walked	9. touched
3. washed	10. worked
4. erased	11. coughed
5. kissed	12. cooked
6. laughed	13. asked
7. stopped	14. helped

GROUP B.

15. snowed	21. enjoyed
16. arrived	22. closed
17. played	23. rained
18. signed	24. sneezed
19. shaved	25. remembered
20. smiled	26. killed

GROUP C.

27. wanted	31. visited
28. needed	32. folded
29. counted	33. waited
30. invited	34. added

◇ PRACTICE 13, p. 110.

1. liked	12. waited
2. closed	13. pointed
3. shaved	14. touched
4. loved	15. melted
5. hated	16. married
6. exercised	17. tried
7. planned	18. hurried
8. dropped	19. replied
9. clapped	20. dried
10. joined	21. stayed
11. shouted	22. delayed

◇ PRACTICE 14, p. 112.

1. counted	7. closed
2. rained	8. yawned
3. helped	9. studied
4. planned	10. worried
5. dreamed	11. dropped
6. erased	

◇ PRACTICE 15, p. 112.

1. finished	7. clapped
2. learned	8. carried
3. tasted	9. rubbed
4. waited	10. stayed . . . cried
5. stopped	11. failed
6. enjoyed	12. smiled

◇ PRACTICE 16, p. 113.

1. last	7. yesterday
2. yesterday	8. ago
3. last	9. ago
4. last	10. ago
5. last	11. yesterday
6. last	12. last

◇ PRACTICE 17, p. 113.

(Note: The time expression can go at the beginning or end of the sentence.)
1. Tim brushed his teeth five minutes ago.
2. Bonnie walked to the park yesterday afternoon.
3. One week ago / Last week, Tom was at home on vacation.
4. Four years ago, Sam graduated from high school.
5. Two days ago / Last Thursday, Jan worked 12 hours.
6. One month ago / Last month, Thomas stayed with his parents.
7. Last night, we watched a DVD.

◇ PRACTICE 18, p. 114.

1. ate	6. ate	11. did
2. ate	7. ate	12. slept
3. ate	8. did	13. slept
4. ate	9. did	14. slept
5. ate	10. did	15. slept

◇ PRACTICE 19, p. 114.

1. get	5. put	9. eat
2. come	6. sleep	10. write
3. go	7. see	11. sit
4. have	8. do	12. stand

◇ PRACTICE 20, p. 115.

1. did	6. ate/had
2. went	7. saw
3. stood/sat/slept	8. got/went/came
4. saw	9. wrote
5. got	10. put

◇ PRACTICE 21, p. 116.

1. didn't come	8. didn't play
2. didn't come	9. didn't answer
3. didn't come	10. didn't see
4. didn't come	11. didn't sleep
5. didn't come	12. didn't do
6. didn't come	13. wasn't
7. didn't play	14. weren't

◇ PRACTICE 22, p. 116.

1. I ate a big dinner last night. OR I didn't eat a big dinner last night.
2. I slept on the floor last night. OR I didn't sleep on the floor last night.
3. I wrote an e-mail last week. OR I didn't write an e-mail last week.
4. I walked to school last month. OR I didn't walk to school last month.
5. I got some money from the bank yesterday. OR I didn't get some money from the bank.
6. I went to my cousins last week. OR I didn't go to my cousins last week.
7. I did some housework yesterday. OR I didn't do some housework yesterday.
8. I worked in the garden yesterday. OR I didn't work in the garden yesterday.
9. I put on my shoes yesterday. OR I didn't put on my shoes yesterday.

◇ PRACTICE 23, p. 117.

1. His alarm clock didn't go off.
2. *(no change)*
3. He didn't cook a big breakfast.
4. He didn't wash the dishes.
5. *(no change)*
6. He didn't see his friends at the bus stop.
7. He wasn't late for work.
8. It wasn't time for work.

◇ PRACTICE 24, p. 118.

1. Did you quit smoking? No, I didn't.
2. Did you eat more healthy foods? No, I didn't
3. Did you exercise three times a week? No, I didn't.
4. Did you take more vacation time? No, I didn't.
5. Did you work seven days a week? Yes, I did.

◇ PRACTICE 25, p. 118.

1. Do they play	6. Did he walk
2. Did they play	7. Does she work
3. Does she play	8. Did she work
4. Did she play	9. Do you like
5. Does he walk	10. Did you like

◇ PRACTICE 26, p. 119.

1. Did
2. Was
3. Did
4. Did
5. Were
6. Did
7. Was
8. Did
9. Were

◇ PRACTICE 27, p. 119.

		Question	*Negative*
1.	a.	Do they play?	They don't play.
	b.	Did they play?	They didn't play.
2.	a.	Do they help?	They don't help.
	b.	Did they help?	They didn't help.
3.	a.	Does she listen?	She doesn't listen.
	b.	Did she listen?	She didn't listen.
4.	a.	Does he work?	He doesn't work.
	b.	Did he work?	He didn't work.
5.	a.	Does the baby cry?	The baby doesn't cry.
	b.	Did the baby cry?	The baby didn't cry.
6.	a.	Are we/you sick?	We aren't sick.
	b.	Were we/you sick?	We weren't sick.

◇ PRACTICE 28, p. 120.

1. A: Were you at home yesterday?
   B: No, I wasn't.
   A: Did you go to a movie?
   B: Yes, I did.
2. A: Is it cold today?
   B: No, it isn't.
3. A: Do you come to class every day?
   B: Yes, I do.
4. A: Was Roberto absent yesterday?
   B: Yes, he was.
5. A: Did Roberto stay home yesterday?
   B: Yes, he did.
6. A: Does your family watch television every day?
   B: No, they don't.
7. A: Is Mohammed in class today?
   B: No, he isn't.
8. A: Was he here yesterday?
   B: Yes, he was.
9. A: Did he come to class the day before yesterday?
   B: Yes, he did.
10. A: Does he come to class every day?
    B: Yes, he does.

◇ PRACTICE 29, p. 120.

1. buy
2. read
3. ride
4. run
5. drink
6. catch
7. drive
8. think
9. bring
10. teach

◇ PRACTICE 30, p. 121.

1. rode
2. taught
3. drove
4. bought
5. bought/drank
6. read
7. ran
8. thought
9. brought
10. caught

◇ PRACTICE 31, p. 121.

1. fly
2. speak
3. take
4. pay
5. wake up
6. break
7. send
8. sing
9. leave
10. meet
11. ring
12. hear

◇ PRACTICE 32, p. 122.

1. flew
2. heard
3. woke
4. took
5. met
6. left
7. rang
8. spoke . . . broke
9. sang
10. sent
11. paid

◇ PRACTICE 33, p. 123.

1. wear
2. say
3. find
4. lose
5. steal
6. hang
7. tell
8. begin
9. sell
10. tear

◇ PRACTICE 34, p. 123.

1. began
2. tore
3. wore
4. told
5. hung
6. said . . . stole
7. lost
8. sold
9. found

◇ PRACTICE 35, p. 124.

1. waited
2. spelled
3. kissed
4. planned
5. joined
6. hoped
7. dropped
8. added
9. pointed
10. patted
11. shouted
12. replied
13. played
14. touched
15. ended
16. danced

◇ PRACTICE 36, p. 124.

1. /t/
2. /d/
3. /t/
4. /əd/
5. /t/
6. /d/
7. /t/
8. /əd/
9. /əd/

◇ PRACTICE 37, p. 125.

1. went . . . bought
2. caught . . . rode . . . got off . . . was
3. ate . . . drank . . . didn't eat
4. asked . . . thought
5. wanted to go . . . stayed
6. read . . . was
7. didn't pass . . . failed
8. drove . . . visited . . . camped . . . went . . . caught . . . didn't catch . . . enjoyed . . . was

◇ PRACTICE 38, p. 126.

1. walks
2. is walking
3. Does Tom walk
4. Do you walk
5. walked
6. saw
7. didn't see
8. Did you see
9. didn't walk . . . took
10. didn't walk

◇ PRACTICE 39, p. 126.

1. didn't finish . . . went
2. isn't standing . . . is sitting
3. isn't . . . was
4. isn't raining . . . stopped
5. didn't go . . . went
6. went . . . didn't enjoy . . . wasn't
7. wrote . . . didn't write
8. didn't come
9. went . . . are sleeping
10. were . . . started . . . didn't arrive
11. asked . . . didn't answer
12. went . . . bought . . . didn't buy
13. woke up . . . went . . . stole . . . took . . . got . . . tore . . . borrowed . . . lost . . . found
14. want to look . . . need to find

NOTES

NOTES